Arab Americans in Michigan

DISCOVERING THE PEOPLES OF MICHIGAN
Arthur W. Helweg, Russell M. Magnaghi, and Linwood H. Cousins, Series Editors

Ethnicity in Michigan: Issues and People
Jack Glazier and Arthur W. Helweg

French Canadians in Michigan
John P. DuLong

African Americans in Michigan
Lewis Walker, Benjamin C. Wilson,
and Linwood H. Cousins

Albanians in Michigan
Frances Trix

Jews in Michigan
Judith Levin Cantor

Amish in Michigan
Gertrude Enders Huntington

Italians in Michigan
Russell M. Magnaghi

Germans in Michigan
Jeremy W. Kilar

Poles in Michigan
Dennis Badaczewski

Dutch in Michigan
Larry ten Harmsel

Asian Indians in Michigan
Arthur W. Helweg

Latinos in Michigan
David A. Badillo

South Slavs in Michigan
Daniel Cetinich

Hungarians in Michigan
Éva V. Huseby-Darvas

Mexicans and Mexican Americans in Michigan
Rudolph Valier Alvarado
and Sonya Yvette Alvarado

Scots in Michigan
Alan T. Forrester

Greeks in Michigan
Stavros K. Frangos

Chaldeans in Michigan
Mary C. Sengstock

Latvians in Michigan
Silvija D. Meija

Arab Americans in Michigan
Rosina J. Hassoun

Discovering the Peoples of Michigan is a series of publications examining the state's rich multicultural heritage. The series makes available an interesting, affordable, and varied collection of books that enables students and lay readers to explore Michigan's ethnic dynamics. A knowledge of the state's rapidly changing multicultural history has far-reaching implications for human relations, education, public policy, and planning. We believe that Discovering the Peoples of Michigan will enhance understanding of the unique contributions that diverse and often unrecognized communities have made to Michigan's history and culture.

Arab Americans in Michigan

Rosina J. Hassoun

Michigan State University Press

East Lansing

⊚ The paper used in this publication meets the minimum requirements
of ANSI/NISO Z39.48-1992 (R 1997) (Permanence of Paper).

Michigan State University Press
East Lansing, Michigan 48823-5245

Printed and bound in the United States of America.
11 10 09 08 07 06 05   1 2 3 4 5 6 7 8 9 10

LIBRARY OF CONGRESS CATALOGING-IN-PUBLICATION DATA
Hassoun, Rosina J.
Arab Americans in Michigan / Rosina J. Hassoun.
p. cm. — (Discovering the peoples of Michigan)
Includes bibliographical references and index.
ISBN 0-87013-667-4 (pbk. : alk. paper)
1. Arab Americans—Michigan—History. 2. Arab Americans—Michigan—
Social conditions. 3. Immigrants—Michigan—History. 4. Michigan—
Ethnic relations. 5. Michigan—Social conditions. I. Title. II. Series.
F575.A65 H37 2003
977.4'004927—dc21
2002153204

Cover design by Ariana Grabec-Dingman
Book design by Sharp Des!gns, Lansing, Michigan
Cover photo: Yakob Na'amen (*left*) and staff, circa 1935.

Michigan State University Press is a member of the Green Press Initiative and is
committed to developing and encouraging ecologically responsible publishing
practices. For more information about the Green Press Initiative and the use of
recycled paper in book publishing, please visit *www.greenpressinitiative.org.*

Visit Michigan State University Press on the World Wide Web at
www.msupress.msu.edu

This book is dedicated in loving memory of my father,
George Phillip Hassoun.

I also dedicate it to my sister,
Lillian Beatrice (Hassoun) Bell for all her support
and help through the years.

ACKNOWLEDGMENTS

I would like to acknowledge all the people in the Arab and Chaldean communities that participated in my research and were supportive of this work. I am grateful to the Arab American Community Center for Economic and Social Services (ACCESS) in Dearborn and my friends in the Chaldean community.

Special thanks also go to Hani Bawardi and the Hani Bawardi Collection, Arab-American Archive Project, Genesee Historical Collections Center, University of Michigan-Flint Library and Archivist Paul Gifford, Helen Samhan and the Arab American Institute Foundation for their statistics, Mrs. Elaine Namen Knox, as well as members of the Lansing Arab-American community. I also thank staff and editors, specifically Kristine Blakeslee, at the Michigan State University Press for their help and patience.

SERIES ACKNOWLEDGMENTS

Discovering the Peoples of Michigan is a series of publications that resulted from the cooperation and effort of many individuals. The people recognized here are not a complete representation, for the list of contributors is too numerous to mention. However, credit must be given to Jeffrey Bonevich, who worked tirelessly with me on contacting people as well as researching and organizing material.

The initial idea for this project came from Mary Erwin, but I must thank Fred Bohm, director of the Michigan State University Press, for seeing the need for this project, for giving it his strong support, and for making publication possible. Also, the tireless efforts of Keith Widder and Elizabeth Demers, senior editors at Michigan State University Press, were vital in bringing DPOM to fruition.

Otto Feinstein and Germaine Strobel of the Michigan Ethnic Heritage Studies Center patiently and willingly provided names for contributors and constantly gave this project their tireless support. Yvonne Lockwood of the Michigan State University Museum has also suggested and advised contributors.

Many of the maps in the series were prepared by Gregory Anderson at the Geographical Information Center (GIS) at Western Michigan University under the directorship of David Dickason. Additional maps have been contributed by Ellen White.

Other authors and organizations provided comments on other aspects of the work. There are many people that were interviewed by the various authors who will remain anonymous. However, they have enabled the story of their group to be told. Unfortunately, their names are not available, but we are grateful for their cooperation.

Most of all, this work is a tribute to the writers who patiently gave their time to write and share their research findings. Their contributions are noted and appreciated. To them goes most of the gratitude.

ARTHUR W. HELWEG, *Series Co-editor*

Contents

Introduction and Demographics

A story is told in the Arab-American community about a Yemeni sailor from Aden, working as a merchant marine on the Great Lakes, who had a chance encounter with Henry Ford, the automobile mogul, in the early 1900s. That chance encounter is said to have started a chain migration of Yemeni Arabs to Dearborn, Michigan. As part of the oral history of Dearborn's Southend, there are several versions of the story about Henry Ford and the Yemeni sailor. In one version, Henry Ford actually is said to have sent a ship to Yemen to pick up workers and bring them to America. There is no evidence that any ship was ever sent—but sometimes word of mouth is as powerful as a boat engine. Word reached Yemen that Mr. Ford was paying five dollars a day to workers in his factory. According to Nasser Baydoun, Henry Ford did bring a small group of Yemenis to work on his iron ore transport ships and in his factory.[1] This may be the origin of the story about a ship going to Yemen.

Whatever version is closest to truth, Henry Ford was looking for manual laborers for the Ford Rouge plant, the largest automobile manufacturing plant in the world at that time. Mr. Ford apparently discovered that Yemen was one of the poorest countries in the world and that the Yemenis had a reputation of being hard workers who were willing to migrate for jobs. At that same time, Henry Ford was beginning to worry about the rise of the labor unions. The Yemenis might have seemed very attractive workers because of the cultural and linguistic barriers that might slow or prevent them from understanding the unions. The Yemenis came, and they worked in the plant side by side with workers from all over the United States and the world. We know they did join the unions. We know that young Yemeni men began coming to work in the factory in the early 1900s—first alone and then decades later with their families to establish the Yemeni-American population in the Southend of Dearborn.[2] The Yemenis were not the only Arabs to arrive in Michigan in the early 1900s. Many Syrian/Lebanese and a few other Arabs and Chaldeans arrived before the first of the Yemenis and were among the first Arab immigrants to make their way to Michigan.

Most Michiganders and other Americans are unaware of the role Arab Americans have played in the automobile industry, not only as factory workers but also as engineers and management. Most people do not think of Arab Americans as a part of the larger automobile manufacturing business. In fact, Arab Americans have entered almost every occupation in the state and have become a part of the fabric of Michigan. Their accomplishments are a matter of pride to the community. Unfortunately, there is also a great deal of misunderstanding, bias, and myth surrounding Arab Americans.

As September 11, 2001, radically changed the lives of all Americans, it also profoundly impacted Arab Americans. It has changed their relations to each other, to other Americans, and to the U.S. government. Before the tragedy, Dearborn's Arab-American community was a source of curiosity to outsiders. After that fateful day, a leaked police report described the community as "a hotbed of terrorism."[3] One event transformed Dearborn in the minds of some people from a quiet suburb with a relatively low crime rate to a den of terrorists. While Arab-American communities might seem like a place where "terrorists" might seek to hide, the reality is that these are the same quiet neighborhoods where Arab Americans have lived for over a hundred years.

If some false media reports made people think Arab people celebrated the attacks, the actual response of the majority of Arab Americans was extreme shock. Arab Americans in Michigan responded to the attacks of September 11, 2001, in a number of ways. Most Arab Americans experienced feelings of grief, fear, horror, shock, and even displaced guilt when they learned of the 9/11 attacks. According to Dr. Adnan Hammad, Director of the Community Health Center for the Arab Community Center for Economic and Social Services (ACCESS) in Dearborn, after the attacks they had to open three additional trauma counseling centers to serve their clients. Michigan (and Dearborn in particular) has a large number of refugees. Many Arab Americans came to this country as refugees who had experienced war and trauma before arriving in the United States. Until September 11, 2001, America was their safe harbor from the violence of the past. The image of the World Trade Towers collapsing, the deaths of so many Americans, including Muslim and Arab Americans, and the thought of such violence coming to the United States triggered post-traumatic stress disorder (PTSD) in many of the refugees in Dearborn. This was largely unreported in the media. ACCESS provided counseling to thousands of Arab Americans in the first weeks after 9/11. In addition, Chaldean organizations also opened their doors to treat the Arab and Chaldean communities for PTSD.

Arab Americans had to face the fear of the backlash, reprisals, and hate crimes. On top of this, the FBI and other government agencies were also targeting their communities. This was not an easy time for the Arabs in America or Michigan. In spite of this, blood donations and support flowed to the victims of 9/11 from the Michigan Arab-American communities.

It is fitting that this monograph be published at this time. It is a crucial period for increasing understanding. For researchers of Arab Americans, September 11, 2001, represents a departure from the past. September 11 marks the beginning of new immigration restrictions for Arabs and Muslims. It changes the pattern of Arab-American immigration and forces us to reevaluate our research assumptions. Arab and Muslim Americans may become the first group targeted for exclusion since the end of World War II. The large numbers of hate crimes that followed in the wake of the World Trade Tower attacks and the anti-terrorist laws that effectively target Arab Americans and Muslims create new conditions for Arab Americans. Individual Arab American

responses to the September 11 attacks and the "War on Terrorism" varied widely, ranging from withdrawal from public places out of fear of
targeting to feelings of extraordinary patriotism. Different Arab-
American communities have also responded differently to the situation. The current situation asks us to review and question the previous
discourse on Arab Americans and demands a more critical study of
local communities and a greater understanding of the diversity and
complexity found in Arab-American culture.

In the wake of the World Trade Tower attacks, Americans will need
greater knowledge of the cultures and languages of Southwest and cen-
tral Asia, North Africa, and the Muslim world. Arab Americans have
valuable resources to offer in the quest for that knowledge. What hap-
pens to Arab Americans and how others treat them tests our national
commitment to pluralism and equality and will determine what kind of
a country America becomes.

This book is not about terrorists; it is about people who have come,
like so many immigrants before them, to the United States to make new
lives for themselves, to contribute to the United States, and to become
Americans. Arab Americans bring their diverse and unique cultural and
linguistic backgrounds to add some bit of Arabic flavor to the larger
salad bowl that is American culture. This discussion will examine who
these people are, their areas of origin, and where and how they settled
in Michigan. In addition to their demographics, the history and settlement patterns in specific cities, as well as some environmental, social,
and cultural issues, will be included.

The Arab Community Center for Economic and Social Services (access)
in Dearborn, Michigan, with its newly opened, $16 million, 38,500-
square-foot Arab American National Museum, has display cases full of
pictures of Arab Americans.[4] The images are of factory line workers
dressed in work clothes smudged with grease and soot, businessmen in
suits, women in their wedding dresses, and even musicians with their
instruments. The pictures illustrate the full gambit of contributions
Arab Americans have made to Michigan and the United States.
Although the popular construction of Arab Americans in the minds of

many Michiganders is of party store or gas station owners, the data show that gas station and party store owners are a minority among all of the occupations filled by Arab Americans.[5] Michigan Arab Americans have helped to build the cars we drive, engineered those cars and other high-tech devices, managed Fortune 500 businesses (one example is Jacque Nasser, former president of Ford Motor Company), and even become congressmen and high-ranking politicians (an example is Spencer Abraham, U.S. secretary of energy). Arab Americans in Michigan have become a part of the weave of the state mosaic. In spite of this, however, they have remained a misunderstood ethnic population in Michigan.

The Arab-American populations in Michigan include a great amount of diversity in national origins, religions, education levels, socioeconomic levels, and degrees of acculturation. The state of Michigan is home to not only one of the largest concentrations of Arab Americans in the United States, but also the most diverse.[6]

Arab Americans constitute one of the largest ethnic populations in the state of Michigan. Michigan is one of the few states that has officially recognized Arab Americans as an ethnic and underserved population.[7] While Arab Americans are currently not classified as an official federal minority, the Michigan Department of Health Office of Minority Health does include Arabs and Chaldeans in their official statistics. According to these estimates, Arab Americans, with a statewide population of at least 408,000 persons of Arab descent, are the third-largest ethnic population in the state of Michigan, after African Americans and Latinos.[8] Zogby International, using the 2000 U.S. Census, places the number of Arab Americans in Michigan closer to 490,000.[9]

According to estimates, there are at least three million Arab Americans in the United States.[10] John Zogby states that Christians comprise 60 percent of the overall Arab-American population. The United States, and Michigan in particular, has experienced an increased influx of Muslim populations since 1952. The difficulty of outreach, the degree of suspicion of questionnaires among immigrants, and their lack of understanding of polling methods are all barriers to obtaining accurate counts of these recent immigrants. Arab Americans were reclassified by the United States Census Bureau from "Turks in Asia" to "Syrians" in the early 1900s and then to "White" after 1952.[11] The re-classification, with current Arab-American counts being folded into those of the white populations, prevents researchers from obtaining accurate modern and historical demographics for Arab Americans. Researchers are doing their best to estimate the population numbers in light of these difficulties. However, the U.S. Census Bureau released information in July 2004, about Arab Americans to the Department of Homeland Security (DHS) broken down by zip code and by country of origin for every U.S. city with an Arab-American population over 1,000. The DHS said they needed the information to put up Arabic signage in airports. This excuse made little sense to the Arab-American community and may further hamper attempts to gain Arab-American cooperation with the census due to fear of internment or persecution. Ironically, at the same time the DHS apologized for having released similar data about Japanese Americans just prior to their internment in camps. Arab-American leaders complained about the data release and the DHS said they would not use the information because it amounted to too much data. This incident may make it much harder for Arab Americans to comply with the census and to obtain accurate counts in the future.

There are several other problems associated with counting Arab Americans. The first problem lies in how to define Arab. An Arab may be defined as someone originating from an Arab country. Formally, an Arab country usually refers to those countries that are members of The League of Arab States. However, the Arab League is a political organization whose membership can fluctuate for political reasons.

The territory covered by the twenty-two current member countries of the Arab League, including Palestine (which is not officially recognized as a state by the United States and most Western countries), spans the area from North Africa, through the Levant (the French colonial designation for the Fertile Crescent), to the Arabian Gulf in southwest Asia.

The Arab world contains significant numbers of ethnic, religious, and linguistic minorities. For example, the Chaldeans and Assyrians consider themselves descendents of the ancient Assyrians of Iraq,

Figure 1. Countries of the Arab World*

AFRICA	ASIA
Algeria	Bahrain
Comoros Islands	Iraq
Djibouti	Jordan
Egypt	Kuwait
Libya	Lebanon
Mauritania	Palestine
Morocco	Oman
Somalia	Qatar
Sudan	Saudi Arabia
Tunisia	Syria
	The United Arab Emirates
	Yemen

*Based on the current membership of the League of Arab States

inheritors of Christian traditions that date to the first century A.D., and speakers of a modern dialect of Aramaic, related to Syriac. Many modern Assyrians and Chaldeans also speak Arabic as a second language. Most Arab Americans also speak English. Many Chaldeans and Assyrians prefer to be considered separate communities and not to be included in counts of Arab Americans. The same may be said of some of the other linguistic, ethnic, and religious minorities, like the Kurds, the Turkomans, the Berbers, the Armenians, certain Southern Sudanese tribal groups, Arab Jewish populations, and so on. There are sizable populations of Christians in Lebanon, Egypt, Syria, and small numbers of Christians in other Arab countries. Some Lebanese, Syrians, Palestinians, and others claim both the Christian faith and Arab roots.

To further complicate matters in the case of the Chaldeans, the Arab and Chaldean Council (the ACC), which is one of the largest Chaldean organizations in Metropolitan Detroit, also serves a sizable population of Arab clients. They are building bridges and reaching out to the Arab community. Estimates of Arab Americans in Michigan differ in whether they include or exclude Chaldeans and other ethnic and religious minorities from the Arab classification. The policy of this author is to be inclusive of all populations in the Arab world, while recognizing the diversity and uniqueness of the ethnic, linguistic, and religious subgroups in the region.

In addition to the difficulty described here in determining who is Arab, the U.S. Census figures for Arab Americans have dramatically under-reported the group, due to the fact that Arab Americans are not an official minority. The 2000 Census included ethnicity on the long form, but the long form was sent to only one out of every seventeen households. Furthermore, as with other immigrant and ethnic populations, many Arab Americans may not have filled out the census forms due to ignorance or fear. In light of this, John Zogby and others have attempted to adjust the census data to provide a more accurate count of Arab Americans. The estimates from the Arab American Institute (AAI) Foundation and the Zogby Institute project Arab-American populations to be three times greater than the census reports. As can be seen in figure 2, Michigan has one of the largest populations of Arab Americans in the United States. Michigan's Arab-American population may no longer be the largest in the country, but it is still the most densely concentrated Arab-American population in the nation.

Demographics of Arab Americans in Michigan

The Arab American Institute (AAI) estimates that there are approximately 490,000 Arab Americans in Michigan.[12] Within the state of Michigan, Arab Americans are heavily concentrated in Southeast Michigan in the Metropolitan Detroit Area. According to AAI estimates, more than 80 percent of state's Arab-American population lives in Macomb, Oakland, and Wayne counties in Metropolitan Detroit. Dearborn, Michigan, has one of the highest densities of Arab Americans both in the state and nationally, with almost one-third of its population claiming some Arab-American ancestry (all data comes from Zogby International and the Arab American Institute and is available at *www.aaiusa.org*).

The concentration of Arab Americans in Southeast Michigan is clearly visible in census maps. The Tri-County Detroit Metropolitan

Figure 2. The Ten States with the Largest Arab-American Populations*

STATE	POPULATION ESTIMATE
California	715,000
Michigan	490,000
New York	405,000
Florida	225,000
New Jersey	240,000
Illinois	220,000
Texas	210,000
Ohio	185,000
Massachusetts	175,000
Pennsylvania	160,000

*See *aaiusa.org/demographics.htm*. Based on 2000 Census data and interpolations by the Arab American Institute Foundation and Zogby International.

Figure 3. The Five Michigan Counties with the Largest Percentages of Arab-American Population

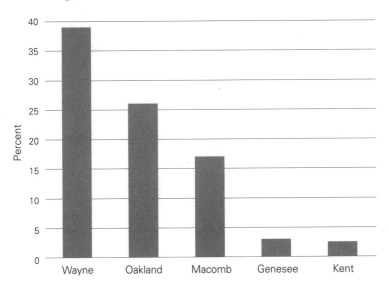

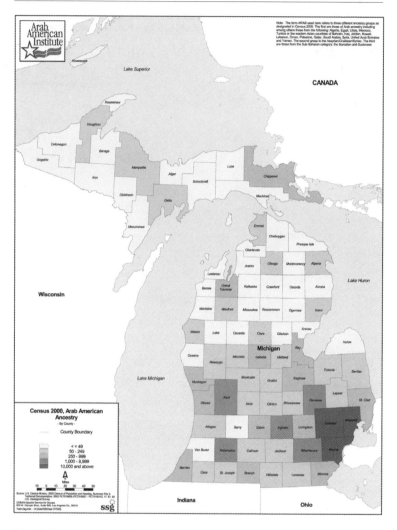

Map 1. Census 2000, Arab Ancestry Reported—Michigan

area contains the highest concentration of Arab Americans in the state
of Michigan and one of the highest concentrations in the United States.
(The key word here is concentration, as Orange County, California,
Washington, D.C., and Chicago all are competing with Michigan for
who has the largest sheer number of Arab Americans.) And nowhere is
there a larger densely concentrated population of Arab Americans than

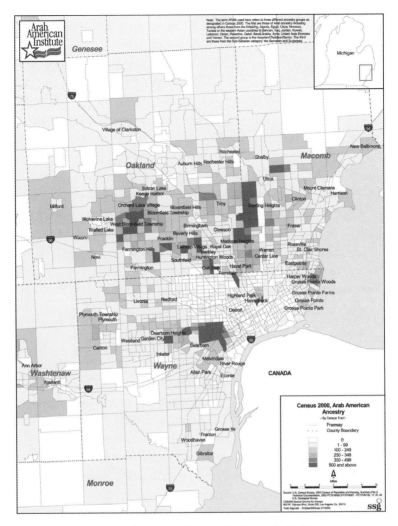

Map 2. Census 2000 Arab Ancestry Reported—Macomb, Oakland, and Wayne Counties, Michigan

in Dearborn, Michigan, and the Detroit Metro area. The Arab-American communities of southeast Michigan also have been the most researched Arab-American communities in the United States by heath, demographic, and social science researchers. The Arab-American communities in Southeast Michigan are some of the oldest in the state, as well, having been founded in the late 1800s.

However, there are other, smaller Arab-American communities in other cities in Michigan. Flint (Genesee County) has a population of approximately seven thousand Arab Americans. The Flint population is predominately made up of Palestinian Christian Arabs from the West Bank and some Christian Lebanese. The Lansing/East Lansing area has a small population of about two thousand predominately Lebanese second-generation Arab Americans as well as some Palestinians.[13] Ann Arbor contains a small but visible group of intellectuals and students among their Arab population. The Ann Arbor community contains Palestinians, Lebanese, and a somewhat diverse student population. Ann Arbor is also home to the University of Michigan's Center for Near Eastern and North African Studies. Grand Rapids also has a small Arab-American community, composed of a small but older Lebanese population, along with an increasingly diverse population of more recent Arab-American immigrants.

Specific Distribution of Southeast Michigan's Arab Population

A study of the density of Arab populations, based on the latest U.S. Census, shows a number of townships within the Oakland-Macomb-Wayne tri-county area that have substantial numbers of Arab Americans. Dearborn has the highest local concentration. Hamtramck has a sizable number of Yemeni workers and some new Iraqi arrivals. The Grosse Point area contains a considerable number of wealthy Arab Americans, including many Arab-American doctors, lawyers, and professionals. Troy and Warren contain a disproportionately larger number of Arab-American engineers, drawn to the engineering firms in these areas. Many of the younger Arab immigrants are engineers who found work with the larger firms located in the northern suburbs of Troy, Warren, and Sterling Heights.

The U.S. Census data has been criticized by Arab community leaders as badly underestimating the overall Arab-American population that is spread into the outer suburbs of Detroit from their densely populated staging areas in Dearborn and Seven Mile.

As noted previously, the Arab-American community is highly concentrated in the Southend and East Dearborn; however, the community is spreading into neighboring areas as witnessed by at least one new Arab-owned restaurant that has successfully developed in the heart of West Dearborn.[14] On the opposite side of Dearborn, there is an expansion of the Dearborn Arab community into Detroit city proper. Arabs (mostly Lebanese) are buying more of the moderately priced homes in the Warrendale area, which, like some areas in Dearborn, was once a predominately Polish area of Detroit.

Other Arabs are scattered throughout the tri-county area.[15] There are older Christian Syrian/Lebanese families spread throughout the Metropolitan area. Christ's Church in downtown Detroit was built at the turn of the twentieth century and had a large Syrian/Lebanese constituency. Although highly acculturated, some of the descendants of the original Syrian families still attend the multi-ethnic parish.[16]

There is a tendency for the more educated Palestinians to live in the northern suburbs. Many of the younger and wealthier Palestinians are engineers starting their own families in the suburbs. Automobile design and high-technology firms in the Warren and Troy area employ the Palestinians. The newer immigrants, and often financially struggling Palestinians as well, live in the Dearborn area or in Livonia. Livonia has a concentration of Palestinian Christians from the West Bank town of Ramallah. Among the Livonia Ramallah population are a number of entrepreneurs of small and middle-sized enterprises.

The Arab population of the Metropolitan Detroit area differs demographically from the national statistics on Arab Americans because of the substantially higher numbers of working-class Arabs in the Detroit area. The Arabs of the Detroit area are also more likely to be living in ethnic communities than are the more affluent and spatially dispersed Arab populations found in other areas of the United States. The Metropolitan Detroit area also contains the greatest diversity in countries of origin, socioeconomic status, and religious backgrounds of any Arab-American population.

The Metropolitan Detroit Arab American population has two major staging areas for new immigrant settlement: the Dearborn Southend community and the Seven Mile/Woodward area. In addition to the two major staging areas, there are several smaller pockets that have higher densities of Arab Americans. Some small pockets of working-class

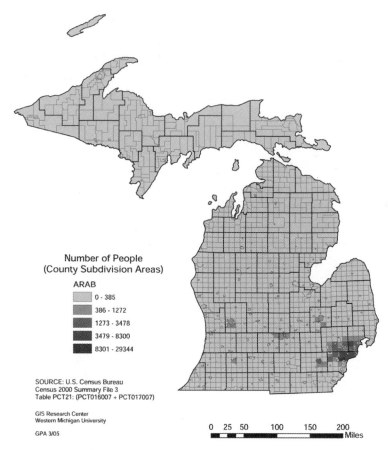

Map 3. Distribution of Michigan's Population Claiming Arab Ancestry, 2000.

neighborhoods occur in neighboring suburbs like Hamtramck, where Yemeni factory workers and unskilled laborers create small, insular neighborhoods.[17]

These working-class neighborhoods contrast with the pattern of Arab-American distributions in the more affluent suburbs. The more northern suburbs of Southfield, Warren, Troy, and Farmington Hills tend to have widely spread populations of more educated, more affluent Arabs and more acculturated second- and third-generation Arab Americans.

In addition to these geographic and socioeconomic divisions in the Detroit Metropolitan Arab population, there is some separation within the community based on religion, ethnicity or country of origin, and to a lesser degree on political factions. Over time there has been a proliferation of Arab and Chaldean social, political, and charitable organizations in the different subcommunities. The degree to which these divisions separate the Arab population is the subject of considerable debate.

The Southend and Seven Mile/Woodward staging areas have been described as separate communities. However, Nabeel Abraham argues that the Arab population of the Metropolitan Detroit area, despite these divisions, contains elements of unification.[18] While it may not be possible to categorize the Arab population in Metropolitan Detroit as a single community, Arab leaders and members of the separate organizations from the various concentrations of Arab population interact both formally and informally. They attend each other's formal gatherings, including annual dinners, socials, weddings, and funerals.[19] Although the Arab and Chaldean social service agencies compete for funding, they also cooperate on a number of projects.

Many of the local Arab radio and TV stations were started by Iraqi Americans. The presence of the local area Arab media may have had some unifying effects. Iraqi music and dance programs spread Iraqi culture in the community in the early 1990s.[20] At the same time, most of the Arabic films are Egyptian. While there were only a small number of Egyptians in the Detroit area, the Egyptian dialect is widely understood because of the films. In addition to the media and the more formal contacts between members of the Arab population, informal networks of friendship weave throughout the communities.

The Origins of Arab Americans in Michigan

Although Arab immigrants in the United States have come from all of the twenty-two Arab-speaking countries, including the Occupied Territories, the majority of Arab Americans have come from the Levantine, or Fertile Crescent area (Lebanon, Syria, Palestine, Jordan, and Iraq), and Yemen.[21] The five major groups of Arab immigrants to the United States are: Lebanese (both Christian and Muslim), Iraqis (including sizable numbers of Christian Chaldeans, Christian Assyrians, and Muslims), Palestinians (Christians and Muslims), Muslim Yemeni, and North Africans (mostly from Egypt, Morocco, and Algeria).

A map of the Arab world or Southwest Asia and North Africa (SWANA) States shows the twenty-two countries that currently belong to the League of Arab States. Note that Turkey and Iran are non-Arab countries that speak Turkish and Farsi (Persian) languages that have Indo-European roots, while having largely Muslim populations. This map omits the Comoros Islands off the coast of East Africa in the Mozambique Channel, a country that is a member state of the Arab League.

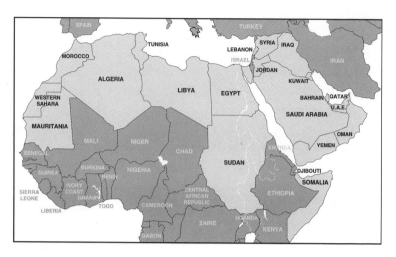

Map 4. The Arab world.

Villages and Pre-Immigration Lifestyles

The majority of Arab Americans in Michigan originated in small towns
and agricultural villages in Southwest Asia. The earliest immigrants
were Syrian/Lebanese Christians from the Mount Lebanon area. Few
studies are available on the Christian mountain villages. The later
Lebanese immigrants were Shi'ites from villages in the south of
Lebanon. Specifically, the majority of the more recent Lebanese immigrants have come from the village of Bint Jebail. There have been a
small number of anthropological studies that describe life in the
Southern Lebanese villages. Emyrs Peters's studies provided a picture of
the social structure and the flavor of life in these villages in the 1950s
and 1960s.[22] Peters's second study refuted the immutable nature of the
social structure of the villages and indicated that the social stratifi-
cation was more mobile than he previously thought. Conditions were
changing rapidly in those villages just prior to the time the majority of
Southern Lebanese immigrated to Detroit.[23]

In addition to the social changes described by Peters, the onset of
the Lebanese civil war brought more upheavals to the South. The self-
sufficient villages of two decades before experienced severe economic

problems. For those who migrated to the United States, a modification of the social class structure of the villages developed. With the migration, social standing in the Detroit area would be determined more by financial success, and to a lesser degree by education, than strictly by traditional kinship relations. Yet kinship does still play a role in determining status in the community.

While many Chaldeans do not identify themselves as Arab Americans, their story as a minority population in the Arab world is very similar to that of other Arab Americans. Almost all of the Chaldeans who immigrated to the Detroit Metropolitan area came from the village of Tel Kaif and some sixteen nearby villages in the mountains of northern Iraq.[24] There are also a small number of Kurds and a few Assyrians from Mosul and the surrounding area of northern Iraq living in the Metro Detroit area. The area of northern Iraq where these groups originated was a major wheat-producing area. Tel Kaif also produced a variety of other agricultural produce, including vegetables and fruits.

Some of the Chaldeans who immigrated resided in Baghdad prior to coming to the United States. The trend of urbanization in the Arab world followed larger general world trends. Between the 1960s and the 1980s, most major Arab and third world cities doubled in size. Baghdad's suburbs grew as migration to the United States increased. The early Chaldean immigrants came seeking greater religious freedom and began arriving long before the rule of Saddam Hussein. Although the Ba'athist party discriminated less against Christians than had previous regimes, the exodus of Chaldeans continued.

The Palestinians in Southwest Michigan came from several villages on the West Bank, primarily Ramallah, El Bireh, and Beit Hanina. Joost Hiltermann describes modern life in Ramallah.[25] Ramallah was once primarily a Christian agricultural village, and the early villagers were largely peasant farmers. Ramallah was also a local center of trade and had a school (actually separate boys' and girls' schools) established by the American Friends (Quakers) during the British colonial period.[26] According to Hilterman, many of the Ramallan villagers defy sociological classification because of the number and types of different work they perform. Economic hardships and landlessness have increased in the village. Some of the Ramallah families found work in the crafts and trades. A few migrated to the Detroit area in the early 1900s, but most came after the creation of the state of Israel.

Members of the Ramallah community of Detroit continue to have close ties to their village, sending money back to their relatives and traveling back and forth for visits. The composition of Ramallah has changed over time. Ramallah today is a sizable town with a majority Muslim population and several nearby refugee camps. Ramallah also serves as a home to the Palestinian National Authority headquarters.

El Bireh is Ramallah's sister town on the West Bank, with a historically Muslim population. The members of the El Bireh community of Detroit also have close ties to their home village, and have their own village association.

In Metropolitan Detroit, members of the Ramallah community have settled heavily in Livonia, where they have established their own village association, or hometown club. The Ramallah population has one of the largest worldwide hometown clubs, with thousands of people gathering each year at their annual conventions. The Ramallans have become entrepreneurs and own a variety of small stores and businesses. Some have become affluent. Like other village groups, the majority of Christian villagers from Ramallah have continued to marry within their original village lineages in the United States.[27]

Comparable stories of villages and small towns come from the Palestinians from Nazareth in Flint, the Lebanese population from the Southern Lebanon village of Deir Mimas that settled in Lansing, and the Palestinian population of refugees from Al-Bassa village now living in the Lansing area.

Understanding General Patterns of Arab Settlement

In general, Arab Americans came to the United States by chain migrations.[28] In this type of migration, the first member of the family to arrive (usually a male family member) will attempt to bring his or her immediate family, other relatives, and friends to the United States. As noted in the author's research, often Arab-American males have brought their parents to the United States, in order to care for them in their old age.[29] Brothers, sisters, and cousins often followed. Most immigrants to the United States have shared this pattern of chain migration. Periodically, U.S. Immigration laws and various push and pull factors change, causing these chain migrations to ebb and flow. A peak wave in U.S. migration occurred in the early 1900s. Until September 2001, the United States was experiencing a second great wave of immigration. Within this broader pattern, different ethnic groups have their own subpatterns. Arab-American immigration patterns have been an area of contention among researchers.

One problem for researchers is the exact dates and cutoff points of the different waves of Arab immigrants. Some researchers fail to emphasize the period between 1924 and 1952 when restrictive immigration laws brought migration from the Arab world to the United States to a virtual standstill. This first period of restriction became more significant after the tragedy of 9/11, when tighter enforcement and restrictions were again imposed on immigrants from the Arab world (and from Muslim countries).

Figure 4 provides a new synopsis of general patterns of immigration of Arab populations to the United States. Arab immigration to Michigan follows the larger general national pattern, with a few unique exceptions. This interpretation of immigration patterns considers three major waves of immigration. Sameer and Nabeel Abraham identified four specific waves of migration in the four major groups of Arab Americans in the Detroit area.[30] Other researchers, like Michael Suleiman, speak of two great waves of Arab-American immigration (1860 to 1948 and 1948 to the present).[31] Because Arab-American studies is a relatively young field of study, with most of its practitioners and theorists currently living, many rich debates and discussions have ensued. The field of Arab-American studies dates to the initial published work of Phillip Hitti in 1924,[32] but the field was not recognized by the mainstream until the 1970s through the research of Barbara Aswad and Mary Sengstock from Wayne State University.

The cutoff dates for the different waves and even the number of waves vary somewhat, according to the researchers. The current analysis could be compared with either a two-wave or three-wave pattern. The pattern given in figure 4 places more emphasis on U.S. immigration laws as cutoff dates for the different waves and reconsiders the significance of the impact of these laws on Arab Americans. It also illustrates the differences between the migrations that came before and after WWI, the wave that arrived in the 1970s and 1980s, and the most recent waves of predominantly Muslim refugee populations. Previous researchers have stressed the dates 1948 and 1967 as cutoff dates for the different waves because of the large numbers of Palestinian refugees created by the establishment of the modern state of Israel in 1948 and the 1967 Arab-Israeli War and the political awareness that these events sparked in Arab Americans. That analysis downplays the significance of the National Immigration Act of 1924 and the change in American immigration with the Immigration Act of 1965 that allowed for a larger number of immigrants and triggered an upswing in influx of immigrants.

Figure 4. General Patterns of Arab-American Immigration

WAVES	COMPOSITION	DATES
First Major Wave	Predominately Lebanese Christians, some Yemeni, Chaldeans, and others.	1860–1924
First Exclusionary Period	The Immigration and Naturalization Act of 1924 excludes nearly all non-European populations, including nearly all "Turks in Asia" or "Syrians."	1924–1952
Second Major Wave	The McCarran-Walter Act, also known as the Immigration and Nationality Act of 1952, opened immigration from the Arab World, but sets low quota for the region. The second wave of Arabs is mostly Levantine Muslims, including more educated "Brian Drain" scholars, engineers, etc., and significant numbers of Palestinian refugees.	1952–1965
Third Wave	The Immigration and Nationality Act Amendments of 1965 removed the quota system but maintained restrictions on immigration. The majority of recent Arab immigrants have been refugees from Palestine, Lebanon, and Iraq, etc., and also include a small new migration of more educated North Africans.	1965–2000
Second (Informal) Exclusionary Period?	Are significant numbers of Muslims and Arabs being imformaly excluded? It is increasingly difficult for Arabs and Muslims to immigrate to the United States with the new regulations after 9/11.	2001–?

Samia El Badry reports that 75 percent of Arab Americans polled in the 1990 U.S. Census reported having arrived in the United States since 1964.[33] The fact that such a high percentage of Arab Americans arrived in America after the mid-1960s strengthens the case for using 1965, with the concurrent change in immigration law that year, to designate the beginning of the next wave (the third wave) of Arab immigrants.

The analysis in figure 4 also considers the fact that the Palestinian refugees created in 1948 were not allowed to enter the United States in significant numbers until after the implementation of the McCarran Walter Act of 1952. The McCarran Walter Act replaced the previous National Immigration Act of 1924 and its exclusionary policy with language that imposed quotas per region of the world.[34] The McCarran Walter Act was less restrictive but continued to secure higher immigration quotas for Europeans, while allowing for set quotas for immigrants from the rest of the world. Later legislation has continued some of these same quotas, with the Arab world being allowed the lowest numbers of immigrants of any world region through the use of limitations per country of origin.[35]

The second wave was predominately Muslim and more highly educated than the first wave. This was certainly the case until the 1980s. In the two studies performed by the author in Michigan and Ohio with surveys of over six hundred individuals, there is a disturbing trend in working-class and new immigrants toward very low education levels.[36] This newer trend is not reflected in the division by some researchers of Arab-American migration into two major waves that does not differentiate the educational differences and the plight of the more recent immigrants.

Recent conflicts in the Middle East appear to have disrupted education at the same time that the region has suffered dismally low regional economic development. This may have significantly harmed education rates in the Arab world in the last few decades. Prior to this time, the Arab world had experienced phenomenal rates of education following independence from the colonial powers. The growth rate of Arab education has suffered setbacks in recent years, however, and this is reflected in the significant numbers of recent Arab immigrants to the United States with only high school, less than high school, or no formal education at all.[37] The latest wave of Arab Americans has been predominantly made up of refugees.

After the tragedy of September 11, 2001, subsequent changes in the implementation of anti-terrorist laws have prevented large numbers of Arabs from immigrating to the United States. Some Arab immigration continues, however, despite the severe restrictions. The year 2001 may therefore mark the cutoff date for the most recent wave of Arab immigrants, depending on what direction the pattern of immigration takes in the future.

Some researchers are interested in demonstrating how subtle changes in economics, regional conflicts, and conditions in immigrants' new country influence their path of acculturation and acceptance into their new lifestyles. Specifically, a group of Canadian researchers studying Arab youth focused more on the cohorts of immigration than on the waves of immigration.[38] As they looked at the different age groups of the children, they noted which generation of migration their parents belonged to and what political and economic conditions shaped their immigration experience. That approach to immigration provides a slightly richer analysis than what has previously been considered in the research on U.S. Arab-American immigration patterns. More research is needed on Arab Americans, and hopefully as the field of Arab-American studies expands, more sophisticated analysis will follow.

Selected Histories by Geographic Areas

Syrian/Lebanese immigrants started arriving in Flint in the early 1900s. Hani Bawardi, in his thesis, recounts the story of three brothers from the Marjayoun area in Southern Lebanon who founded three separate dynastic families in Flint: the Joseph, Salim, and Barakat families.[39] However, Palestinian Christians from the town of Nazareth were also among the early Arab immigrants to Flint. Ameen Farah, a Nazarene, arrived in Flint in 1914, by way of Egypt and Syracuse, New York.[40] Ameen Farah was an important political activist who attempted to mobilize the Arab-American population against the Ottoman Turks during WWI and to raise their awareness of the history and culture of Greater Syria (the Lebanon, Palestine, Syria, Jordan area during the Ottoman period).[41] Although he was briefly in the grocery business and his family members went on to found a family business dynasty in Flint, Ameen Farah's activism was his greater contribution to Flint and to Arab-American history.[42]

Hani Bawardi reports that seven other Nazarenes, seeking to avoid conscription into the Ottoman Turkish army (which they feared would be a death sentence for Christians), arrived in Flint in 1917. By that time, Arab Americans, mostly from southern Lebanon, were also living in

Ameen Farah (center), circa 1918. Courtesy of Roy Farah, The Bawardi Collection, Arab-American Archive Project, Genesee Historical Collections Center, University of Michigan–Flint Library.

Fenton and Burton, Michigan—including the Sweidan, Bu-Asali, and Sefa families.[43]

The early Arab-American community in Flint was divided religiously and politically—mostly into Lebanese Maronite Catholics and Palestinian Orthodox Christians. Today, the churches in the community, Our Lady of Lebanon Maronite Church and St. George's Antiochian Orthodox Church, cater to the spiritual needs of this generation of Arab Americans in Flint.

Only in the last few decades has Flint developed a sizable Muslim population, with at least two mosques within the city limits. The Muslim community felt compelled to locate their new Islamic Center outside the city limits, however, due to space considerations and what

American Druze Foundation Founding Members. Courtesy of The Bawardi Collection, Arab-American Archive Project, Genesee Historical Collections Center, University of Michigan–Flint Library.

at least one community member said were matters of prejudice. The architecture and design of the spacious new Islamic Center is of pride to the community. Arabs are a sizable part of the Muslim community in Flint, but as in other places, the Muslim population of Flint is diverse, including African Americans and immigrant Muslims from many countries.

In addition, Flint is the birthplace of the American Druze Foundation. The Druze belong to a separate religion, said to have originally developed as an offshoot from Islam but now a very distinct religion whose followers are found mostly in Lebanon, with some Druze in Syria and among the Palestinians. The Hamady family, with others in Flint, founded the Druze Foundation headquartered in that city.

Perhaps the best known of the Arab-American families in Flint is the Hamady family. The Hamady brothers started a push-cart business in the 1920s that later grew into one of the largest supermarket chains in Flint.[44] Kamal Hamady founded the Hamady Supermarket downtown. Jack Hamady is still a remembered, beloved, and well-respected

Jack Hamady Family, Early Years (above) *and Later Years* (right). *Courtesy of The Bawardi Collection, Arab-American Archive Project, Genesee Historical Collections Center, University of Michigan–Flint Library.*

humanitarian in the Flint area. School libraries, youth sports teams, and dozens of humanitarian programs have been named in honor of Jack Hamady and the Hamady family.

A small Arab town developed in Flint in the 1920s and 1930s that was bounded by Industrial Avenue and South Saginaw and was centered at the intersection of Water and Saginaw Streets.[45] A fixture of this community was a coffeehouse owned by the Rizik family called "Little Syria," where men smoked the *argeeleh*, the water pipe, and drank thick Arabic coffee. In the 1920s and 1930s Arab Americans from Flint served in World War I and worked in the factories. They were a part of almost every aspect of life in Flint.

When people talk about the 1930s, the great sit-down strike of 1936–37 is remembered. For forty-four days, ending on February 11, 1937, workers in the three General Motors plants in Flint conducted a sit-down strike, effectively stopping all work on the car manufacturing lines.[46] The oral history of the community includes accounts of the strike. Some Arab Americans working at the plants participated in the strike, while nearby Arab-American restaurant owners, acting in solidarity with the striking workers, helped smuggle food to the strikers.[47] Arab Americans have lived through the closing of the many of the factories in Flint and the economic woes of the city.

As Hani Bawardi points out, Arab Americans in the Flint area have been in the grocery business for ninety-two years, and in some cases there is third- and fourth-generation store ownership. Many of these stores are in predominately African American neighborhoods, and this has placed them in a difficult position in terms of relations with the African American community.

The author, Rosina Hassoun, lived in Flint and worked in conjunction with the Genesee County Health Department in 1997–98 on the Genesee County Children's Immunization Coalition. The local health department was also working to curb underage cigarette smoking, in part by stopping local storeowners from selling or giving tobacco products to minors. The local merchants, like those the author studied in the Cleveland area, are heavy smokers who started smoking as children.[48] Smoking is a problem in the national Arab-American population and it includes: lack of awareness or internalization of the health

Elizabeth Mansur Delling Family. Courtesy of The Bawardi Collection, Arab-American Archive Project, Genesee Historical Collections Center, University of Michigan– Flint Library.

ramifications of smoking; underage smoking in the case of Arab males; hidden smoking among females (it is seen as unfeminine by some Arab Americans); the cultural use of the *argeeleh,* or water pipe; and possibly one of the highest rates of tobacco use of any ethnic population in the United States (these are estimates based on small studies such as the author's in the absence of national statistics).

Some of the storeowners saw the efforts by the health department as entrapment, bias against them, and targeting of Arab storekeepers. The African American community, on their side, could not understand the insular nature of the Arab family structure. Many of the grocers wanted better relations with the African American community but did not know how to achieve this. When the author asked one African American religious community leader what he thought could be done about relations between the two communities, he said, "You have to be willing to come and drink at my kitchen table from my cracked cup." The history of the economic disempowerment of African

Americans is mostly unknown and little understood by many Arab-American storeowners. Getting both communities to sit together over coffee in an informal setting appears to be a good idea.

In Flint, as in Detroit, although the bulk of the storeowners may be Arab or Chaldean, the majority of the members of the Arab-American community there are not storeowners. The younger generations are going off to universities, and many of them may not return to Flint. The Arab-American population in Flint today is estimated at approximately seven thousand.[49] The Arab-American community in Flint appears to be rather stable in numbers, but Flint's difficult economic situation and slow recovery will surely impact the decisions of the next generation of young people, Arab or non-Arab, to stay in or leave the area.

The Greater Lansing Arab-American Population

As in other cities, the first immigrants to the Lansing area were over-whelmingly Syrian/Lebanese Christians. Even today, Lebanese Americans comprise the greater portion of the Arab-American community in the Lansing/ East Lansing area. The total Arab-American community in Lansing may number as many as two thousand people, but no clear local numbers are available.

The history of the Lansing area Arab Americans is somewhat unique. In the late 1800s, Lebanese Christians from the village of Deir Mimas in the Marjayoun district of southern Lebanon began immi-grating to the United States and found their way to Lansing to work in the Oldsmobile Plant and the Diamond Reo Truck factory.[50] Perhaps the first Arab American to immigrate to the Lansing area was Sam Soloman in 1897. He began a road construction company that over the years did a great deal of work for the State of Michigan.

Some of the other early Lebanese immigrants opened small gro-cery and liquor stores. The second generation (born in America) were better educated, and many entered professional fields. The original Syrian/Lebanese community in Lansing was composed of a few neigh-borhoods near the Oldsmobile plant. One person who lived in those neighborhoods recounted walking from her neighborhood to St. Mary's church in downtown Lansing on Sundays.

*Kamil F. Adado (*back row in hat*), Reo Motor Company, Lansing, Michigan, 1920. Courtesy of family.*

Deir Mimas, where the bulk of the early immigrants to the Lansing area originated, is a small agricultural village in the mountains of Lebanon. The village, now growing into a town, is known locally for its production of grapes, but also produces wheat, olives, and vegetables. Historically, they traded wheat to Bedouins for donkeys and lamb. The village also sold their produce to both Lebanese and Palestinians in this border area of Lebanon. The village has sent people to America for approximately 120 years, and there are fourth-generation descendents of Deir Mimas in the Lansing area. Many of these Lebanese Americans still own houses "back home" in Deir Mimas, and they regularly send money home to their village. Lebanese American money recently built a new city hall, and the Lebanese American community in Lansing has also funded other projects for the poor in Deir Mimas.

The story is told that the first of the people from Deir Mimas to arrive in the United States found work "on the great railroad West." The first Deir Mimas families "landed" in Carney, Nebraska, and started potato farming. Members of the Lansing community are still in touch with their Carney cousins, and they often meet up in the village in Lebanon, where they routinely send·their children so that they can

learn about their origins and language. There are thousands of descendents of Deir Mimas in the United States today. Each year in Lansing
there is a picnic of the Deir Mimas families attended by three to four
hundred people. The descendents from Deir Mimas still tend to prefer
to marry within their village lineages.

In addition to Deir Mimas, Deir Dagae'eh, a nearby village, has also
sent a few families to the Lansing area. In addition, a few Lebanese from
other villages, like Bint Jebeil and Tibnien, also came to Lansing in the
1900s. These families are as fiercely proud of their villages, as are the
people of Deir Mimas. The great debate among Arab-American
researchers remains the degree to which early Arab American immigrants, and specifically the Lebanese, assimilated. The case of the
Lansing area Lebanese clearly demonstrates that this population, while
very proudly American (including a number of U.S. veterans), did not
totally assimilate. They acculturated, and adapted to life in America, as
Americans, but retained a good portion of their original culture. Their
continuous ties to their place of origin illustrate their transnationalism.

Some of the prominent Arab-American families in the Lansing area
include the Saad (Saad Furs), Rahail, Shaheen (automobile sales),
Adado, Kalouch, and Toubia families. Wadih (Woody) Zamel is locally
known for starting the South Cedar Bakery in 1981, and then in 1984
beginning what would become a small chain of Woody's Oasis restaurants that are popular with students and others. He retired from the
restaurant business in 1999. Another Arab-American family has opened
the most upscale Arabic restaurant in East Lansing, Sultan's restaurant.
There are also a few other Arab-American restaurants in the Lansing/
East Lansing area.

The Eyde family, also Christian Lebanese, are a prominent family
in real estate. Perhaps the most well known Lansing Arab American is
Senator Spencer Abraham, who is proudly claimed by local people as a
descendent of Deir Dagae'eh. The Farhat family, specifically Leo Farhat
and Leo Farhat Jr., have been politically active on the Lansing City
Council and in the Republican Party.

In addition to the first wave of Lebanese Americans to the Lansing
area, there was a smaller wave of Palestinians from the village of Al
Bassa. They claim that the name Al Bassa is an old Canaanite word and

that this village had very ancient origins. The village of Al Bassa was north of Acre and until 1925 was part of Lebanon. When the boundaries of Lebanon and Palestine were redrawn by the British, the village was included in Palestine, as part of the Galilee. The village of Al Bassa, according to its former residents, was about 40 percent Muslim and 60 percent Christian, with at least two churches and a local mosque. Israeli forces destroyed the village, and descendents today tell their story of ethnic cleansing, and of how their village is now a place where animals graze inside what is left of the mosque. Walid Khalidi documented the destruction of the village in his book *All That Remains* with photographic evidence.[51] Al Bassa was taken by Hagannah forces in Operation Ben Ami on May 18, 1948 and within a week most of its inhabitants were expelled into Lebanon.

About 95 percent of the population of Al Bassa were displaced outside historical Palestine and made refugees, with the majority ending up in the Dbayeh refugee camp east of Beirut. Today the camp still has a population of some 4,223 people, mostly Christian refugees.[52] During the Lebanese civil war (beginning in the late 1960s) the population of the Dbayeh camp found themselves in the middle of the war. Their camp suffered severe damage during the war and this sent waves of Al Bassa refugees fleeing, and eventually a group of families came to Lansing, Michigan. Like the Ramallans of the West Bank and other villagers, the Al Bassa families have an international village club and they also have an annual picnic or gathering in Lansing each year attended by over three hundred people. In addition, they still tend to marry within their village group. The local eastern-rite church, St Joseph's Melkite Catholic Church, is the religious home of many of both the Lebanese and the Palestinians.

The early Lansing Arab Americans were religiously diverse, including Catholics, Orthodox, and a few Protestants. The early community attempted to start their own church in the nearby town of Charlotte, but the distance to the church was too far. About twenty-five years ago, their current church, St. Joseph's Melkite Church, was established on Mt. Hope Road. Although an Eastern Catholic–rite church, the parishioners have a broad background, some having originally been Melkite

Catholics, some Eastern Orthodox, and even a few Protestant converts. There is also an Eastern Orthodox church in East Lansing that has a few Arab-American attendees.

In addition to the Christian Arab-American population, there is a small and growing Muslim community in East Lansing that has grown up to serve Michigan State University's diverse Muslim population. Arab Americans comprise only about 30 percent of the East Lansing Muslim population.

The current Islamic Society of Greater Lansing grew from the Muslim Students Association at Michigan State University, when the numbers of attendees at Friday prayer grew to over 150 (180 by 1979).[53] The students and local Muslims established the Islamic Center, which includes a mosque and an Islamic school near the university campus. Just after the tragic events of 9/11, someone fired shots into the adjacent house of the caretaker of the mosque.[54] The university, local law enforcement, and others rallied around the Muslim community following that incident. The Muslim community, although shaken by this hate crime, continues to recover and grow. The Islamic Center appears to include a highly educated, diverse, and sincere population of Muslims that is slowly growing over time.

This may be the first written history of the Greater Lansing Arab-American population. Undoubtedly, more research on this community is needed.

Arab Americans in Ann Arbor

While there is new research into the political activism of the first wave of Arab immigrants, the Arab-American community in Ann Arbor has the unique distinction of being the birthplace of modern Arab-American national political organizing. The Ann Arbor Arab-American community has a long history of scholarly activism. The Association of Arab American University Graduates (AAUG) was born in the basement of an Arab-American professor's home in Ann Arbor. The AAUG would become the first modern national Arab-American association and one of the longest-lived Arab-American scholarly organizations, surviving for more than thirty years. In August 1967, a group of mostly academics met in the basement of sociologist and public health researcher Dr. Rashid Bashshur to create a scholarly national organization that would present Arab perspectives to the American public.[55] The group of founding AAUG intellectuals grew to include Dr. Fawzi Najjar from rival Michigan State University, Dr. Ibrahim Abu-Lughud from Northwestern University, Arab-American lawyer and activist Abdeen Jabara, and many others.[56]

The AAUG was the premiere Arab-American scholarly organization for over thirty years and the oldest Arab-American national organization in the United States until its recent demise in the late 1990s due to funding problems. There are current efforts to revive the organization. The AAUG published a peer-reviewed journal and was the epicenter of Arab-American intellectualism during its long life. The organization moved to the East Coast and often held annual meetings in the Washington, D.C., area.

Today the Arab-American community in Ann Arbor is still best known for its students, activists, scholars, and culture creatives (innovators, creative individuals including artists, musicians, etc.). There is a small but significant number of Palestinians, both Muslim and Christian, in Ann Arbor. There are also a few Lebanese, Egyptians, and other Arabs, many of them a result of the brain drain from the Arab world. Most of the scholars are professors at the University of Michigan in the fields of engineering and medicine. Many of Ann Arbor's Arab-American scientists, engineers, and medical researchers are pioneers in their fields, producing internationally recognized research.

The University of Michigan, Ann Arbor, has a long-established Center for Near Eastern and North African Studies and an internationally recognized Arabic language program that has drawn Arab and Arab-American students to the campus. The Arab-American students at the University of Michigan have been among the most organized and vocal in the nation in discussing and defending Arab human rights.

There is also a substantial and diverse Muslim community centered around the university. When a local Islamic leader, Rabia Haddad, was detained after 9/11, the community rallied around him and his family but they were unable to prevent his deportation. The community still maintains his innocence. The Ann Arbor Muslim community is one of the most highly educated communities in the United States.

The Ann Arbor Arab-American community regularly hosts creative Arab-American artists like Simon Shaheen, an internationally recognized composer and master of the Arabian lute, the oud, and the violin. Arab-American writers like Anton Shammas, Palestinian novelist, essayist, playwright, poet, and literary translator, have found a home in Ann Arbor. The Greater Detroit area is still the cultural center of Michigan's Arab-American population, but Ann Arbor serves as a special area within the larger Michigan population.

A more comprehensive history of the early Arab-American community in Ann Arbor and a more thorough listing of the scientific, scholarly, and literary contributions of the Ann Arbor Arab-American community should be an area for future research.

Arab Americans in Grand Rapids

There are efforts under way to collect an oral history of Grand Rapid's Arab Americans. To date, only a general history is available. There is a mention in an early history of Grand Rapids of a "small colony of Syrian immigrants" there in the late 1800s or early 1900s.[57] According to the web site of the Russian Antiochian Orthodox Church, St. John Crysostom, St. George's (Syrian) Orthodox Church was founded before 1914, possibly in 1908.[58] The early Syrian and Lebanese community may also have contained a number of Catholics as well. There was an early Syrian/Lebanese community with at least one Arab-American band that played traditional music at community gatherings.

The Arab-American community in Grand Rapids has grown in size and diversity. West Michigan has reportedly experienced a growth in its Muslim population from two thousand to ten thousand in recent decades, although the Muslim community includes large numbers of Bosnians, Pakistanis, and other non-Arab Muslims.[59] Today, the Grand Rapids Arab-American community is religiously diverse. There are at least two mosques in Grand Rapids, including the Islamic Center of Grand Rapids. The Arab-American community now includes people from a variety of Arab countries. Grand Rapids has recently experienced a slight influx of Sudanese, as have other cities in Michigan, although many of them are from the non-Arab areas of Southern Sudan. The Grand Rapids Arab-American community is small, but continues to grow in size.

The History of Arab Immigration to Southeast Michigan

Although the two historical staging areas for Arab migration in Metropolitan Detroit (Dearborn's Southend and the Seven Mile/Woodward area) date back to the original founding of the Arab and Chaldean populations in Detroit, there has been considerable fluidity in the settlement patterns within the tri-county area over the last century of Arab migration. In the Metropolitan Detroit tri-county Arab-American population, Arab regionalism and nationalism (country of origin), kinship, and to some degree religion all have influenced the settlement patterns. The socioeconomic status of the immigrants and access to employment, however, have often outweighed these other considerations as to choice of where to live. Village identities also have played a role in settlement patterns, although divisions in the Arab populations tend to be more social than geographic.

The staging areas in the Southend and Seven Mile/Woodward are survivors of an earlier era when ethnic communities in the United States tended to form isolated ethnic enclaves in larger cities. The Metropolitan Detroit area has several of these older communities, including Greek Town and Mexican Town. These other two ethnic communities have become very successful in drawing tourists and other Detroit residents to their restaurants and shops. The Arab community has been less successful in drawing clients from the larger metropolitan area; however, the newer Arab restaurants in East and West Dearborn may be an exception. Dearborn Arab organizations are attempting to increase tourism and to attract customers from other areas of the Detroit metropolis.

Specific Historic Settlement Patterns within the Greater Detroit Metropolitan Area

The local waves of immigration in Southeast Michigan differ somewhat from the generalized patterns of Arab immigration to the United States. As with the national pattern, the earliest Arab migrants to the Detroit area were Syrian/Lebanese Christians. The first Arab immigrants to Detroit were Lebanese men seeking employment. The first Muslims settled in Highland Park, near the Ford Motor company plant where many of them worked. The first Palestinians arrived between 1908 and 1913 and were Muslim. Chaldeans first came to Detroit between 1910 and 1912, before the establishment of modern Iraq as a state.[60]

Although some Yemenis arrived in the Detroit area as early as 1900, they established a real presence in the Detroit area between 1920 and 1925.[61] Initially, only Yemeni men came, as temporary workers, leaving their wives and families in Yemen. It was not until the late 1960s that Yemeni families began immigrating permanently to the Dearborn Southend. This first wave of Arab immigrants arrived at a time when the city of Detroit was just beginning to be transformed into an industrial center of the United States. Arab immigrants found work in the auto industry and as door-to-door salesmen (peddlers) in the budding metropolis.

The later immigrants of this wave of Arab immigrants to Detroit arrived to find very different circumstances. They had survived the hardships and famines of World War I in the Middle East and subsequently lived through the Great Depression in the United States. Some nine thousand Lebanese villagers arrived in Detroit from 1930 to 1938.[62]

The vast majority of the second wave of Arab immigrants did not arrive until 1952, after the National Immigration and Naturalization Act of 1924 was effectively repealed by new legislation. This wave contained

Iraqi American Yakob Na'aman in front of his store in Detroit (Bush and Warren St.), circa 1937. Courtesy of Mrs. Elaine Namen Knox.

increasing numbers of Arab Muslims and large numbers of Palestinian refugees. The third wave of migrants to the Detroit area were better-educated Arabs. During this period, Detroit underwent a transformation. Large numbers of African Americans from the South began arriving in Detroit in search of work. There was a massive "white flight" from the inner city and the development of predominately white suburbs surrounding the city.[63] Red lining (a practice by real estate agents and banks of excluding certain buyers by selectively showing them houses in only one are of town or by denying them loans based on prejudice) was a common occurrence, and Arabs in some cases were considered white and welcomed.[64] In other areas, like Dearborn, Arabs were seen by some as unwanted intruders. The city and its suburbs still struggle for mutual reconciliation and acceptance.

The Arab immigrants that arrived in Detroit from 1967 to 1990 included Arabs escaping the Lebanese and Yemeni civil wars. After 1967, Yemenis began bringing their families, and the Yemeni Southend community was established in earnest. After the occupation of the West Bank, another wave of Palestinian migrants came to Detroit. Many

Palestinians found themselves stateless and were forced to accept permanent exile. Detroit provided a place of employment and refuge for Palestinians seeking a new life.

Yemenis in the Detroit area came from what once were North and South Yemen, as well as the Hadramaut area that partially lies in a mountainous area on the border of the formerly two Yemens.[65] The recent unification that followed the civil war in Yemen had the impact of healing some of the divisions in the Yemeni population in Detroit, although there has always been some intermarriage between Yemenis in Detroit from North and South Yemen.

Following the Lebanese civil war and the 1983 Israeli invasion of Lebanon, large numbers of Southern Lebanese settled in East Dearborn.[66] These new Shi'ite Lebanese immigrants settled in East Dearborn and established a number of small businesses and restaurants along Warren Avenue. This development resulted in a rebirth of the economically depressed area. In 2001, the Southern Lebanese community in Dearborn celebrated the Israeli withdrawal from their original villages. For several days and nights, there was a carnival-like atmosphere in East Dearborn. It demonstrated the ties the Arab-American immigrants still have to their relatives and villages in the Middle East. While Southern Lebanon was under Israeli rule, Lebanese Americans sent money back to their villages of origin in Southern Lebanon, supporting villages like Bint Jebail. Many of the Arab villages could not have survived without this income from relatives.

The most recent arrivals in the Michigan Arab-American population are Iraqi refugees. The majority of these refugees are Shi'a from the south and Kurds and others from northern Iraq. A large number of these refugees were individuals who allied themselves with the United States against Saddam Hussein or were part of the population that rebelled against Saddam Hussein in southern Iraq. They were expelled from Iraq, and many of them found themselves in refugee camps in Turkey and in Saudi Arabia.

The United States and European countries accepted refugees from these camps for almost a decade. The refugees from some of these camps reported mistreatment in the form of torture and rape. Other refugees are skilled and educated professionals that are in need of work and recertification. The U.S. Office of Refugee Resettlement has been coordinating the efforts to provide services for the refugees.[67] Most were placed into the U.S. welfare system and given two years' assistance to find jobs, learn English, and obtain education and recertification—a very daunting and nearly impossible task in so short a time.

Many of the children from these camps suffered trauma and had no education. The United States initially attempted to spread out the three thousand Iraqi refugees accepted annually into the United States into different areas of the country. The lack of services available to them and their desire to live in Arab communities, however, created an internal migration of these refugees to Michigan.

Dearborn's Southend

Barbara Aswad described the Dearborn Southend area as a separate and distinct community.[68] Dearborn's Southend is isolated in a heavy industrial area that is cut off from the rest of Dearborn and southwest Detroit by freeways and manufacturing plants. The Southend was historically a multiethnic working-class area designed to provide living space for workers at the Ford Rouge Plant and nearby factories.[69] The Southend contains one of the oldest industrial residential communities in the United States, with houses surrounded by the Ford Rouge Plant and other automobile-related factories.

Today, the population of the Southend is composed primarily of Arab Muslim working-class families. The Southend population is predominately Yemeni, with some Lebanese, a few Palestinians, some recently arrived Iraqi refugees, and a small number of non-Arab families.[70]

Because the Southend area lies "in the shadow of the Ford Rouge Plant" and is nestled in a highly industrialized, economically depressed area of the city, environmental pollution, high unemployment, and low socioeconomic status plague the Southend community. The plant layoffs during the 1980s caused extensive economic hardships for the Southend popuation. The area began to show some signs of financial recovery in the early 1990s but appears to be stagnated at the current time. The families in the Southend have persisted in spite of the financial problems in building a unique and close community.

The main commercial area of the Southend, along Dix and Vernor Avenues, is lined with small Arab businesses, an Arab coffeehouse or two, a few Arab restaurants, and a mosque. The owners of these businesses cooperated in redesigning the exterior of the buildings along the main strip, through the use of façades, constructing Arabic arches and domes. The idea was to create an "Arab town" atmosphere that would bring tourists to the area. However, economic recovery is slow in coming to these neighborhoods. Each business along the strip has Arabic and English signs advertising its goods. ACCESS, the Arab Center for Economic and Social Services, has its main office complex located on a side street very near the main economic strip in the heart of the Southend.

The streets of the Southend are lined with small one- and two-story houses, most built during the 1920s and 1930s. The houses have tiny yards, and there are only small spaces between the brick and wooden-frame homes. They are very similar in construction to the typical factory row houses that date to the same period.[71] Coal shoots are visible on the outside of many of the houses, confirming the period of their construction. In the spring and summer, families sit out on the front porches of their houses in the evenings and the streets are constantly filled with Arab children, playing games and walking. Yemeni men and women can be seen wearing their brightly colored traditional clothing—although one sees the full gambit of clothes, from very traditional to very westernized dress, in the community. The brightly colored clothing of the Yemeni contrast sharply with the black body veiling of some of the new Iraqi Shi'a from southern Iraq. Their darker clothing seems to symbolize the hardships they suffered when they rioted against Saddam Hussein and fled as refugees to Saudi Arabia and Turkey. Many of the Iraqi refugees were incarcerated in concentration camp-like conditions in Saudi Arabia before arriving in the United States. The Iraqis seem to keep to themselves.

The religious sectarian differences in the community (the Yemeni Muslims are Sunni and the Iraqi and Lebanese are Shi'a) appear to be of lesser importance than the differences in their countries of origin. There are a number of village and hometown clubs among the Palestinians (such as the Beit Hanina Club in the Southend), and many separate men's and women's groups among the Lebanese, Palestinians and Yemenis.

The one large park (La Peer Park) in the area sports a swimming pool that is full of Arab boys (usually only boys due to modesty and religious traditions) during the summer. In the cool of the summer evenings, mothers pushing strollers and families taking walks are common in the park. Grilling food and picnics are very popular pastimes during the summer months, and the yards and the park are favorite places for this informal dining.

In the winter, these same neighborhoods seem forlorn. During the colder months, children who may not have warm coats due to their poverty may don several layers of clothing to keep warm, and the traditional Yemeni dress appears inadequate to protect against the cold. Few people venture out except for necessities, but instead visit their neighbors indoors.

Dearborn's Southend is geographically more isolated than other communities, due to the factories and the Rouge River that make access to the area a little more difficult. This may have helped to isolate the area from change. In addition, the concentration of large numbers of newly immigrated, very traditional, and nonacculturated Yemenis in the Southend community has added to this feeling of insulation from change. The Yemeni population of the Southend are very proud of their community and the progress they have made, in spite of the economic challenges they face.

East Dearborn

East Dearborn and the Southend were originally designed by Henry Ford to be the working-class areas of the town near the Ford Rouge Plant. Eest Dearborn was separated from West Dearborn by a greenbelt that is today filled in by a huge shopping mall. West Dearborn, until the recent incursion by upscale Arab restaurants, was almost exclusively non-Arab. The older Polish, Italian, and Eastern European populations that once inhabited East Dearborn and the Southend fled those areas over time. This left the Southend and East Dearborn predominately Arab. Although distinctly different, it is difficult to separate East

Dearborn and Dearborn's Southend, since the populations of these two areas form intricate networks of friendships and business associations. There are some differences, however, both in composition and in socioeconomic levels between these two areas of Dearborn. Since the late 1970s, East Dearborn has experienced a massive influx of Lebanese Shi'a from Southern Lebanon. At the same time, the Warren Avenue area in East Dearborn has experienced a development boom of small · Arab-owned businesses and restaurants.

The biggest thrust of that development has come with the expansion of Arab-owned businesses since the early 1980s, growing from a mere half dozen to over sixty businesses along Warren Avenue alone.[72] Collectively, Arab Dearborn (East Dearborn and the strip malls in the Southend) has more than thirty Arabic restaurants, approximately eight Arabic pastry shops and bakeries, and a variety of shops selling Arabic specialty items and imports.[73]

The neighborhoods in East Dearborn vary from lower- to middle-class neighborhoods. Many streets in East Dearborn have only Arab owners and renters. Women hanging out clothing in the summer gossip over the back fences in Arabic, and Arabic music often blares from houses and cars. In the evenings, the younger, more affluent youth (both boys and girls) cruise Warren Avenue in their same-sex groups in cars, reminiscent of the American adolescent behavior that characterized the 1950s.

The rapid increase in the number of immigrants in Dearborn in the 1980s brought about urban renewal along Warren Avenue, but taxed the ability of the city's school system and other public services to cope with a new language and cultural group. Dearborn's school-aged population was estimated at approximately 32 percent Arab in 1994 (including the Southend, East Dearborn, and West Dearborn), and the percentage may be even higher now.[74] The Dearborn Public Schools, in conjunction with the Arab Community Center for Economic and Social Services (ACCESS), implemented special bilingual education programs, parent education programs, and even media outreach geared toward helping the Arabic community.[75] Some of those plans for bilingual education met with heavy opposition from some non-Arab community members and the Dearborn School Board, which had no elected Arab-American members. The struggle for higher MEAP (Michigan standardized tests) scores and better bilingual (Arabic-English) education continues.

The Seven Mile/Woodward Area

The Seven Mile/Woodward area is comparable to Dearborn's Southend in some ways. The Seven Mile/Woodward area contains a small Chaldean Christian population, surrounded by an economically depressed area with a largely African American population. Members of the Chaldean community in this area belong to a Christian population originally from the mountains of northern Iraq. Chaldeans were originally Aramaic-speaking Eastern Rite Catholic Christians from a number of villages around the city of Mosul. The question of Chaldean identity has fascinated researchers.

Mary Sengstock, in focusing on the degree of identification of the Chaldeans as Arabs, argued that the Chaldeans constitute a separate community.[76] According to Sengstock, many of the older Chaldeans, who still speak Chaldean, a modern dialect of Aramaic, continue to identify as Chaldeans. More recent immigrants from Iraq, although still originating from the area around the village of Tel Kaif in northern Iraq, are more Arabized and tend to speak Arabic more frequently than they do Chaldean. Some of the later Chaldean immigrants may also identify themselves as Arabs. The younger Chaldean generations often speak only English, while maintaining the ability to understand some Chaldean and Arabic from their parents and grandparents.

There have been periods of cooperation and interaction between the Chaldean and Arab communities in Greater Detroit. This has generally occurred when the Arab and Chaldean populations have perceived an outside threat, like the discrimination they experienced during the Gulf War in 1991. The Southend Arabic press and the major social service agencies, such as the Arab Community Center for Economic and Social Services, rallied with the Iraqi community at this time, as the entire Arab population in the city experienced a rise in hate crimes aimed at Arabs. [77] While it may be too soon to determine a long-term trend, September 11, 2001, may have caused some rifts between the religious communities, but the pressure of hate crimes perpetrated by Americans who cannot distinguish Sikhs and South Asians from Arabs, let alone Muslims from Christians, indicates that the communities may have to come together for mutual support. The two largest social service organizations serving Arab, Chaldean, and other populations in the metropolitan area, the Arab and Chaldean Council and the Arab Community Center for Economic and Social Services (ACCESS), both serve diverse and sometimes overlapping populations.

The Chaldean population contains a large number of small entrepreneurs who own gas stations, grocery stores, and party or convenience stores in the Seven Mile area. The Seven Mile/Woodward area, bordering the African American area, with the placement of the party stores and gas stations in predominately African American communities, has brought the Chaldean store and gas station owners into direct conflict with the African American community. These struggling communities compete for the scarce resources in this area, and it has deepened the severity of their problems.[78] Numerous attempts have been made to reconcile the Chaldean-, Arab-, and African American populations and to stop the violence that has resulted in the deaths of storeowners and African American youths alike.

Chaldeans who are able to attain a higher socioeconomic status have a tendency to move out of the Seven Mile/Woodward area. As a result, an affluent Chaldean community has developed in Southfield and Farmington Hills. The Chaldeans in these affluent suburbs are engaged in entrepreneurship and professional careers.

Special Topics Concerning
Arab Americans in Michigan

Environmental Issues

The climate and environment of Michigan differ greatly from those of the original homelands of Detroit's Arab immigrants. The climate of Detroit, with its cold, snowy winters and relatively mild, humid summers, is a radical departure from the Mediterranean climate. Many Arabs complain that they dislike the cold and snow and miss the mild climate that allowed them to walk outside year-round.[79]

Detroit is a highly urbanized, industrialized city. Although massive efforts have been made to help the financial recovery of the city, Detroit has been severely affected by the cutbacks in the auto industry since the 1980s.

While many Detroiters may feel that the problems and crime rate of the city have been exaggerated, life in a large city in America is radically different from life in a small village or town in the Arab world. The pace of life in the city is much faster than that of the rural villages of the Arab world. The Arab immigrants to Metropolitan Detroit have had to make large adjustments to a new Western, urban lifestyle.

The same high pollution levels that trouble other industrialized areas of America also plague the city of Detroit. The Dearborn Southend area is especially hard hit, as it is a noncontainment area (the State of

Michigan and the EPA allows certain parts of the State to exceed the air quality standards in special non-containment areas that benefit business in those zones) for air pollution, and the Arab population endures a range of the pollutants from the Ford Rouge Plant and at least a dozen other large factories in the same area.[80] The heavy truck traffic in the area also adds more air pollution to the the community's burden, and especially the steaming slag trucks from the factory. The city of Detroit and many of the older suburbs also have lead pipes that contribute to lead contamination of the water, and lead paints are common in the older houses. Initial research of a sample of three hundred Arab Americans in Metropolitan Detroit showed a high rate of severe and chronic respiratory problems, including asthma in young children, among the Arab community in the Southend when compared with Arabs and Chaldeans living in other parts of the city.[81]

The Seven Mile/Woodward area is considered to be a high crime area and is a financially stressed area. The location near the Southfield freeway also probably increases air pollution in that area. Abandoned buildings, run-down businesses, and empty lots plague this area of Detroit.

Arab Americans in the northern suburbs live in an environment with less crime and pollution. These affluent neighborhoods sport manicured lawns, executive apartment buildings, high-rise businesses, fancy restaurants, and mostly clean industry. Not all of the Arabs in these areas live in luxury, but more of the Arabs in the suburbs have middle- and upper-class incomes.

Arab-American Culture, Family, Gender, Food, and Health

Contrary to the stereotypes of Arabs, there are a variety of lifestyles, clothing styles, and degrees of freedom for women, and also a great diversity, in the Arab world. That diversity is also present in Arab-American communities in the United States. It translates to differences in lifestyles, family practices, and acceptance of or resistance to acculturation or assimilation.

In general, Arab-American culture tends to be very family centered. Although-Arab American families are becoming smaller and more nuclear with time in the United States, the basic Arab-American family is an extended family, often with multiple family members contributing to the income of the family. The extended family household provides financial and emotional support for the family.[82]

Some families, both Christian and Muslim, practice semi-arranged marriages. Mothers play a role in helping to arrange marriages, and, at least in the ideal form, the prospective bride and groom have the right to refuse the marriage arrangements. In practice, degrees of family and peer pressure exist. However, significant and increasing numbers of Arab, Chaldean, and Muslim women and men are completely free to choose their own partners.

Arab-American gender roles are also changing over time. The changes in gender roles are influenced by county of origin, area of origin (urban versus rural), degree of education, and time in the United States. Research conducted by the author shows that Arab-American women in Michigan are increasingly using their buying power and receiving educations. Arab-American males are also increasingly sharing household chores, like cooking and child care, with their spouses.[83]

The process of acculturation for most immigrant groups is a time of increased intergenerational conflict. This is particularly true for Arab Americans. The children of the new immigrants are exposed to television and peer pressures at school and normally acquire English language skills faster than their parents. Debates over issues like dating can be quite intense in some families. In general, the culture dictates respect for parents and the elderly.

The common cultural characteristics, in addition to a focus on the family, include a respect for generosity and hospitality. Every visitor to an Arab-American home (or often even a business) will be provided with coffee or tea and something to eat. It is considered rude to refuse such hospitality. Arabic food is an important component of generosity.

The majority of the Arab restaurants in Michigan serve Lebanese (and some Palestinian) style cuisine. Americans are becoming familiar with foods like shish kabobs, Arabic bread, stuffed grape leaves, and tabbouleh salad. When Arab Americans have guests, meat is a high-status food, so dishes of baked and grilled lamb are commonly served.

Fewer non-Arabs are familiar with Iraqi and Yemeni traditional dishes or with the common meat and vegetable stews (*yaknas*) that are served over rice and bread at home.

When Arabic food is consumed in the proper serving sizes, red meat is limited, and a good exercise regimen is followed, traditional Arab-American food is very healthy. The USDA has proposed a healthy food pyramid based on the Mediterranean diet. Therefore, lessons from the Arab-American community are important for all of us. Studies conducted by the author indicate that when exercise is reduced and red meat, fats, and sweets are added to the traditional Arab village diet, the results are unhealthy.[84]

There have been no macro or large-scale health studies on Arab Americans, but the author's studies and other small scale studies show that diabetes, hypertension, cardiovascular disease, high cholesterol, and obesity in later years may be problems for Arab Americans.[85] Like Latinos, African Americans, Native Americans, and most new migrants to industrialized cities, Arab Americans may be especially susceptible to these diseases of acculturation, stress, and dietary and lifestyle change. In addition, smoking rates among Arab Americans may be among the highest of any ethnic population, and higher than the mainstream. According to the author's research in Michigan and Ohio, Arab Americans may be smoking at rates approaching 45 percent or more (there have been no large-scale tobacco studies, so this is an estimate from smaller studies). Arab Americans also have a tendency to start smoking at a younger age.[86]

Arab Americans may be facing a challenging future in the United States and in Michigan. The stresses on their communities are enormous at this particular time. Arab Americans have a strong presence and have made Michigan home for multiple generations. The Arab-American communities are full of young people who know no other home but Michigan. They are faced with both pressures to adapt and acculturate and the expectation that they will preserve their traditional culture. The result is a modification of culture over time.

Acculturation: Subsequent Generations of Arab Americans in Michigan

Almost all the studies and information on Arab Americans in Michigan have focused on the newer immigrants, mostly in Southeast Michigan. The piece of the story that is most often missing is what happened to Arab Americans in the second, third, fourth, and now some in the fifth generation. In Flint and the Greater Lansing area, where the Arab-American communities are smaller and easier to locate, it is possible to find the subsequent generations. In Southeast Michigan, in the suburbs of the large Detroit Metropolitan area, locating the subsequent generations is difficult. Many have blended into mainstream American society. Others, like the people from Deir Mimas and Ramallah, have changed and acculturated but remained close to their heritage and connected to their village or hometown identities.

Although data is lacking, the general trend appears to be that the Arabic language is not often maintained after the second generation.[87] Arabic language maintenance has become important to the security of the United States and for understanding this culture. The loss of the Arabic language in subsequent generations is of concern to all Americans. Traditional foods and certain ethnic religious rituals may be preserved longer in subsequent generations.

The second, third, and fourth generations of Arab Americans invariably have benefited from better education. Education is highly valued in the children of the first wave and in Arab culture in general. The children of this first wave went on to become professionals in almost every field of study. The pattern of acculturation in Arab Americans follow a trajectory that is similar to that followed by Italian and other immigrants in America. Furthermore, because acculturation is a two-way phenomenon, Arab Americans have added something to the fabric of American culture. Of course, food is the most recognizable contribution. Arabic flat bread, tabouleh salad, hummus, and stuffed grape leaves are all becoming supermarket fare.

Other contributions of this community to American culture are harder to measure. Arab Americans, as one of the largest ethnic populations in the state of Michigan, contribute to the state in taxes, services, and productivity. Arab Americans in Michigan teach children, heal

Michigan's sick, and design, operate, and build businesses. Nearly everywhere you look, there is an Arab American at work. The challenge for scholars studying Arab Americans is to document the contributions and lives of the subsequent generations of Arab Americans in Michigan.

Summary

From the first early Syrian/Lebanese seeking work in door-to-door sales and the first Yemeni to encounter Henry Ford and work in the automobile factories to the most recent Arab immigrants, Arab Americans have been a part of Michigan history for over a hundred years.

The tragedy of September 11, 2001, unfortunately caused many Americans to become suspicious of the Arab-American community, while the shock of the attacks caused trauma in an Arab-American community already full of refugees suffering from post-traumatic stress syndrome. For Arab Americans who saw America as their safe haven from the problems of the Middle East, the tragedy of September 11 and the aftermath of profiling and targeting have had profound impacts. As a result, there is a need to understand Arab Americans and their history in Michigan.

Today Arab Americans constitute the third-largest ethnic population in Michigan, after African Americans and Latinos, with an estimated 490,000 members in the communities.[88] Macomb, Oakland, and Wayne Counties in Southeast Michigan contain up to 80 percent of the Arab-American population in Michigan. Genesee and Kent Counties also have significant Arab-American populations.

Arab-American settlement patterns have changed over time, but Dearborn and the Seven-Mile/Woodward areas in the Greater Metropolitan Detroit area are traditional immigrant staging areas that have attracted large numbers of new Arab and Chaldean immigrants. The Dearborn Arab-American population is expanding into neighboring areas of Detroit. There is also a tendency for more affluent Arab Americans to move to or settle in the northern suburbs of the metropolis.

Arab Americans in the Metropolitan Detroit area may originate from any one of the twenty-two countries that are members of the Arab League. However, the majority of Arab Americans in Michigan are from five subgroups: Syrian/Lebanese, Iraqis and Chaldeans, Palestinians, Yemenis, and North Africans (mostly Egyptians, Moroccans, and Tunisians). The vast majority of the Arab Americans in Michigan originated from agricultural villages and small towns, including Bint Jebail, the Marjayoun area, Tel Kaif, Ramallah, Beit Hanina, Deir Mimas, and the Hadramaut.

Arab-American immigrants have arrived in several different waves, with each wave drawing from a distinct population and having a unique reason for immigrating. There were at least two major waves of immigration. The first was predominately made up of Syrian/Lebanese Christians, but also included Yemeni migrant workers and some early Chaldean immigrants. The second wave of immigration has largely been made up of refugees, but also includes some highly educated Arabs, as part of the ongoing brain drain from the Arab World. The second wave has included Palestinian refugees, Lebanese Shi'a, Yemenis, and in the most recent wave, Iraqi refugees—all seeking to escape the conflicts in the Arab world.

In examining the specific histories of settlement in different parts of the state, each city in the state has its own variation on the general pattern. For example, Flint's Arab-American population began arriving in the early 1900s and contained sizable numbers of both Syrian/Lebanese and Palestinian Nazarene (from the town of Nazareth) Christians. In addition, the American Druze Foundation was established in Flint. The Druze belong to a distinct religion and are mostly found in Lebanon and in the Galilee. The diverse (Arab and non-Arab) Muslim population in Flint includes many more recent immigrants.

There is a long history (over ninety-two years) of Arab store ownership in Flint.

The Greater Lansing area was initially settled by Syrian/Lebanese, and Lebanese still constitute the largest segment of the area's Arab-American population, including second-, third-, and fourth-generation Arab Americans. A second, smaller wave of Palestinians originally from the village of Al Bassa, by way of Dbayeh refugee camp in Lebanon, also found a home in Flint. The Lebanese from the village of Deir Mimas have maintained multigenerational ties to their village of origin while acculturating to an American lifestyle.

Ann Arbor has an Arab-American population centered around the University of Michigan campus that includes a significant number of scholars and professionals. Ann Arbor has also become a center for cultural creativity, with artists and writers like Anton Shamas residing there. The first modern and longest-lived national Arab-American scholarly organization, the Association of Arab-American University Graduates, was founded in Ann Arbor.

The Grand Rapids area was also initially settled by Syrian/Lebanese in the early 1900s. A small "Syrian colony" developed in Grand Rapids that centered around the Orthodox churches. Southwest Michigan has subsequently developed a diverse and rapidly growing population of Arab and non-Arab Muslims.

Southeast Michigan was an early recipient of Syrian/Lebanese immigrants, who settled initially in the downtown Detroit area and moved to the suburbs over time. Early Muslim Arab populations, specifically the Yemenis, settled in Highland Park and then the Southard area of Dearborn and Hamtramck. The Chaldeans began arriving in the early 1900s, settling in the Seven Mile/Woodward area and later moving to more affluent areas like Farmington Hills. Palestinians from Ramallah began arriving during the first wave of immigration, settling in Livonia. Dearborn's Southard neighborhoods began as diverse multicultural working-class neighborhoods and have become almost predominately Yemeni over time. The east side of Dearborn saw large influxes of Lebanese Shi'a, starting with the onset of the civil war in Lebanon in the 1960s and again with the Israeli invasion of Southern Lebanon in the early 1980s.

Over time, Dearborn's Arab-American population has continued to grow and has expanded into neighboring areas of Detroit. At least one upscale Arab-American restaurant can currently be found in West Dearborn. Southeast Michigan, particularly the Metropolitan Detroit area experienced an influx of Iraqi refugees and some highly educated North Africans in the last decade. This has added to the diversity of the Arab-American community. Southeast Michigan remains the cultural center of Arab-American life in Michigan and contains numerous social service agencies, like the Arab Community Center for Economic and Social Services (access) and the Arab and Chaldean Council (ACC), as well as hosting numerous social, religious, and cultural organizations.

Arab Americans in Michigan practice a variety of lifestyles that reflect differing levels of acculturation in the areas of culture, gender roles, and health. The diversity in the Arab world in countries of origin, urban versus rural background, and education levels translates into differences in Arab Americans and their acculturation in the United States

In general, Arab Americans tend to be very family oriented and to have extended families. There appears to be a trend toward nuclear families over multiple generations in the United States. The author's research shows that gender roles among Arab-American families are changing over time, with more women acquiring education and buying power and more men sharing in household chores, like cooking.

Marriage for both Muslim and Christian Arabs is traditionally semi-arranged, with parents playing a large part in partner selection, but where ideally both parties have the right to refuse an arrangement. In practice, this may vary. In Arab-American immigrant families (as with most new immigrants), differences in acculturation and English language acquisition between parents and children can intensify intergenerational conflicts. In general, Arab-American culture values family unity, parents, and the elderly.

In addition, Arab Americans value generosity and hospitality, and that value dictates offering coffee, tea, and food to guests. Non-Arab Americans are usually most familiar with Lebanese cuisine, as it is served in most Arab restaurants. The common everyday foods, like the vegetable and meat stews (*yakna*) usually served at home, are less well known to non-Arab Americans. In its traditional form, Arabic food is quite healthy, being rich in vitamins and fresh vegetables and fruits. However, Arab-American diets, according to the author's research, appear to be changing over time in the United States, with the introduction of snack foods, fast foods, sweets, more salt, and fats. Arab Americans also appear to be getting less exercise than their counterparts in the Arab world. Health problems for Arab Americans may include high risk for diabetes, hypertension, cardiovascular disease, high cholesterol, and obesity. In addition, Arab Americans have very high rates of smoking. Furthermore, many Arab Americans are experiencing high levels of stress that accompany acculturation and lifestyle changes and that were heightened after the attacks of September 11, 2001, and the subsequent backlash and profiling.

Most of the research on Arab Americans has focused on new immigrants. Very little is known about the second, third, fourth, and fifth generations of Arab Americans. Arabic language maintenance appears to be a problem in subsequent generations. As with other ethnic populations, educational advantages and financial opportunities in America have provided economic advancement and increased the contributions of multiple generations of Arab Americans to Michigan's economy and culture. Arab Americans have become an indelible part of Michigan's history and society.

A Gift from the Hassoun Family to the People of Michigan

A Family Recipe for Making Genuine Hummus Bit Tahini, taken from *The ABC's of Middle Eastern Cooking,* by George P. and L. Louise Hassoun (Camas, Wash.: Bellgraphics, 1989).

Garbanzo (Chick Pea) Dip (Hummus Bit Tahini)

1½ cups dried chick peas
pinch of bicarbonate
4 Tbsp. parsley
3 cloves (sections) of garlic mashed together with 1 tsp. salt.
½ cup lemon juice
½ cup tahini (from health food or Arabic store)
4 Tbsp. olive oil
paprika

Clean and wash chick peas in a colander under cold running water. Cover with water to spare. Add a pinch of bicarbonate and let soak for twelve hours. Drain and place peas in a heavy pan. Cover again with water. Bring to boil on high heat, then lower the setting and let simmer until the peas are soft and mash readily between your fingers. Strain the peas, reserving a cup of liquid. (Two 16-oz. cans of cooked garbanzo beans could be used in lieu of the dried chick peas; boil until tender before using, approximately twenty minutes.) Chop the parsley finely and combine the other ingredients except the olive oil and paprika in a food processor until mashed into a thin paste. If too dry, add up to one cup of the reserved liquid until the mixture has the consistency of a thin peanut butter. Stir in 1 tablespoon of the chopped parsley. Spread on a flat platter, and clean and raise the edge all around. Sprinkle remaining parsley on top. Decorate with a dash of paprika, then pour the oil on top (advice from the author: go easy on the oil if you are watching calories). Serve with Arabic pocket bread, pickles, green onions, and olives.

Variations: Ground lamb (seasoned with Allspice, black pepper, and salt or Arabic five spice mixtures) and pine nuts sautéed in butter may be poured over the top in lieu of olive oil.

Enjoy!

Resources

Organizations

- Arab Community Center for Economic and Social Services (ACCESS), 6451 Schaeffer Dr., Dearborn, MI 48120; phone: (313) 945-8380.
- ACCESS Main Office, 1651 Saulino Ct., Dearborn, MI 48120; phone: (313) 842-7010.
- Arab American and Chaldean Council, 28551 Southfield Rd., Lathrup Village, MI 48076; phone: (248) 559-1990.
- Arab American Heritage Council, 1000 Beach St., Flint, MI 48502; phone: (810) 235-ARAB.
- A compendium of resources on Arab Americans in the Metropolitan Detroit area is available on-line at *www.theaanm.org.*

Video

- *Tales from Arab Detroit,* directed by filmmaker Joan Mandell. Olive Branch Productions and Arab Community Center for Economic and Social Services.

Museums

- The Arab American National Museum (AANM), the first Arab-American museum in the United States, is located at 13624 Michigan Ave., Dearborn, MI 48126. The telephone number is (313) 582-AANM (2266), and the e-mail is *aanm@accesscommunity.org.*
- The Arab Community Center for Economic and Social Services (ACCESS), the sponsoring organization of the AANM, also has maintained some museum artifacts at their main building located at 3651 Sauline Ct., Dearborn, MI 48120.

Notes

1. Paul Hughes, "Selling Arab-America to the Tourism Industry: Efforts Underway to Take Advantage of Large Population Concentrations," *Arab American Business*, August 2001. On-line version available at http://www.arabamericanbusiness.com/issue10_august/marketing.htm.

2. Nabeel Abraham, "The Yemeni Immigrant Community of Detroit: Background, Emigration, and Community," in *Arabs in the New World: Studies on Arab-American Communities*, ed. S. Abraham and Nabeel Abraham (Detroit: Center for Urban Studies, Wayne State University, 1983), 109–34.

3. Chris Christoff, "Police Report: Apology on the way for Stirring Fear, Bias," *Detroit Free Press*, October 25, 2001.

4. Anan Ameri and Yvonne Lockwood, *Arab Americans in Metro Detroit: A Pictorial History* (Chicago: Arcadia Publishing, 2001).

5. John Zogby, *Arab America Today: A Demographic Profile of Arab Americans* (Washington, D.C.: Arab American Institute, 1990).

6. Paul Gaurilovich, "Detroit's Arab-American Community Is North America's Largest," *Detroit Free Press*, 18 October 1990, 2E.

7. Michigan Department of Public Health, *Minority Health in Michigan* (Lansing: Michigan Department of Public Health, 1988).

8. See http://www.aaiusa.org/demographics.htm.

9. The Arab American Institute (AAI) and John Zogby have supplemented the U.S. 2000 Census undercounts with their own polling information to arrive at the estimate of 490,000 Arab Americans in Michigan. The estimate of 250,000–300,000 Arab Americans in the Metropolitan Detroit area alone had been used without updating them for about a decade prior this new estimate. See http://www.aaiusa.org/demographics.htm.

10. Zogby, *Arab America Today.*

11. Helen Hatam Samhan, "Not Quite White: Race Classification and the Arab-American Experience," in *Arabs in America: Building a New Future,* ed. Michael W. Suleiman (Phialdelphia: Temple University Press, 1999), 209–26.

12. See note 9.

13. These are estimates by the author based on interviews with people in the communities in Flint and the Lansing area. Accurate counts do not exist for these areas.

14. Rosina Hassoun, *Dearborn Arab-American Community Restaurant and Tourist Guide* (Dearborn: Ford Motor Company and the Michigan Equity Program and the City of Dearborn with the Arab Community Center for Economic and Social Services, 1994).

15. A more extensive description of the Arab American settlement patterns is available in: Gary David, *The Mosaic of Middle Eastern Community in Metropolitan Detroit* (Detroit: United Way Community Services, 1998). Unfortunately, the report is currently out-of-print.

16. Participant observations by author; see Rosina Hassoun, "Bioanthropological Perspective of Hypertension in Arab American in Metropolitan Detroit" (Ph.D. diss., University of Florida, 1995).

17. Participant observation, see Hassoun, "Bioanthropological Perspective."

18. Sameer Abraham, "Community in Metropolitan Detroit," in *The Arab World and Arab Americans: Understanding a Neglected Minority,* ed. Sameer Abraham and Nabeel Abraham (Detroit: Wayne State University Center for Urban Studies, 1981), 22–33.

19. Participant observation: the author observed numerous formal occasions attended by members of the various communities between 1993 and the present. Community organizations hold annual dinners and invite leadership and members from all Arab American subgroups. The ACCESS annual dinner is an example.

20. While the author conducted her doctoral dissertation, she observed local television programs and listened to local radio stations.

21. The following texts and articles provide overview information on Arab Americans: Ernest McCarus, ed., *The Development of Arab American Identity* (Ann Arbor: University of Michigan Press, 1994); Gregory Orfalea, *Before the Flames: Quest for the History of Arab Americans* (Austin: University of Texas Press, 1988).

22. Emyrs L. Peters, "Aspects of Rank and Status among Muslims in Lebanese Villages," in *Mediterranean Countrymen*, ed. J. Pitt-Rivers (The Hague: Mouton, 1963).

23. Emyrs L. Peters, "Shifts in Power in a Lebanese Village," in *Rural Politics and Change in the Middle East*, ed. Richard Antoun and E. Harik (Bloomington: Indiana University Press, 1972).

24. Mary C. Sengstock, "Traditional and Nationalist Identity in a Christian Arab Community," *Sociologist Analysis* 35 (1974): 201–10.

25. Joost Hiltermann, "Abu Jamal: A Palestinian Urban Villager," in *Labor and the Women's Movement in the Occupied Territories*, ed. E. Burke (Princeton, N.J.: Princeton University Press, 1991), 364–67.

26. The author's Arab grandmother taught in the girls' school in Ramallah, her father was educated in the Friend's school there, and her Iowa Quaker mother served in the American Friends Service Committee in Acre in 1952.

27. Confidant information. Interview by R. Hassoun, Detroit, Mich., 1994.

28. Roger Daniels and Otis L. Graham, *Debating American Immigration, 1882–Present* (Boulder, Colo.: Rowman and Littlefield Publishers, 2001).

29. Rosina Hassoun, *The Greater Cleveland Arab-American Needs Assessment Final Report* (Cleveland: Arab-American Community Center For Economic and Social Services in Ohio [AACCESS-Ohio], 2001).

30. S. Abraham, "Detroit's Arab-American Community: A Survey of Diversity and Commonality," in *Arabs in the New World: Studies on Arab American Communities*, ed. S. Abraham and Nabeel Abraham (Detroit: Center for Urban Studies, Wayne State University, 1983), 84–86.

31. Michael W. Suleiman, "Introduction: The Arab American Immigrant Experience," in *Arabs in America: Building a New Future*, ed. Michael W. Suleiman (Philadelphia: Temple University Press, 1999), 1–21.

32. Phillip Hitti, *The Syrians in America* (New York: George H. Doran, 1924).

33. S. El Badry, "The Arab American Market," *American Demographics* 16(1): 22–30.

34. Samhan, "Not Quite White," 209–26.

35. El Badry, "The Arab American Market," 22–30.

36. See Hassoun, "Greater Cleveland Arab-American Needs Assessment," 17–22; Hassoun, "Bioanthropological Perspective," 121–29.

37. Hassoun, "Greater Cleveland Arab-American Needs Assessment."

38. Sharon McIrvin Abu-Laban and Baha Abu-Laban, "Teens Between: The Public and Private Spheres of Arab-Canadian Adolescents," in *Arabs in America: Building a New Future*, ed. Michael W. Suleiman (Philadelphia: Temple University Press, 1999), 113–28.

39. Hani Bawardi, "Arab Immigrants in Flint, Michigan: The Case of Merchants in the Inner City" (Master's Thesis University of Michigan, 1997), 8–9.

40. Ibid.

41. From the finding aid, *Bawardi Collection*, Arab-American Archive Project, Genesee Historical Collections Center, University of Michigan–Flint Library. See the Ameen Farah papers.

42. Hani Bawardi personal interview Oct. 18, 2004. Also see note 41.

43. Ibid.

44. Ibid.

45. Ibid.

46. This web site, maintained by the Walter P. Reuther Library at Wayne State University, has pictures and a description of the great Sit-down Strike, including a picture of people passing food to the strikers. Arab American restaurant owners sent food into the factories for the strikers in solidarity with the strike. http://www.reuther.wayne.edu/exhibits/sitdown.html.

47. The story of how the restaurant owners helped the strikers was told to the author several times by community members.

48. Hassoun, "Greater Cleveland Arab-American Needs Assessment," 33–40.

49. Members in the community estimate the Arab-American community to number around seven thousand, but no official count is available.

50. The oral history of the Lansing/East Lansing Arab-American community was based on interviews collected by Rosina Hassoun, most conducted in January 2004, but also some local knowledge was gained by living in the area and interacting with the local Arab-American community.

51. Walid Khalidi, ed., *All That Remains: The Palestinian Villages Occupied and*

Depopulated by Israel in 1948 (Berkeley: University of California Press, 1992), 6–9 (note: the photo of the village of Al-Bassa is on page 7).

52. UNRWA, the United Nations Relief and Works Agency, provides current numbers and condition of the Palestinian refugees from the Galilee in the Dbayeh refugee camp on their web site, http://www.un.org/unrwa/refugees/lebanon/dbayeh.html.

53. This information came from a personal interview and from The Islamic Society of Greater Lansing Handbook, written in 1998, published by the Islamic Center and available for visitors to the mosque.

54. The shooting targeting the home of the caretaker of the mosque in East Lansing was reported to the U.S. Commission on Civil Rights as a hate crime. See http://www.usccr.gov/pubs/tragedy/imm1012/zogby3.htm.

55. Janice J. Terry, "Community and Political Activism among Arab Americans in Detroit," in *Arabs in America: Building a New Future*, ed. Michael W. Suleiman (Philadelphia: Temple University Press, 1999), 241–54.

56. Ibid.

57. William J. Etten, *A Citizen's History of Grand Rapids* (Grand Rapids, Mich.: A. P. Johnson for the Campau Centennial Committee, 1926), available on-line at http://www.rootsweb.com/~mikent/etten1926/cosmopolitan.html.

58. The web site of the Russian church, St. John Chrysostom Antiochian Church, in Grand Rapids, Michigan, is found at http://www.3saints.com/stjohn-history.html. St. George's Antiochian Church also has a web site at http://www.antiochian.org/midwest/Parishes/St_George_GrandRapids.htm.

59. *The Grand Rapids Press*, 17 December 2000, reported an increase in the Muslim population of West Michigan.

60. Sengstock, "Traditional and Nationalist Identity in a Christian Arab Community."

61. Abraham, "Yemeni Immigrant Community."

62. Ibid.

63. J. T. Darden, R. C. Hill, and J. Thomas, *Detroit: Race and Uneven Development* (Philadelphia: Temple University Press, 1987).

64. Ibid.

65. Abraham, "Yemeni Immigrant Community."

66. S. Y. Abraham, Nabeel Abraham, and Barbara Aswad, "The Southend: An Arab Muslim Working-Class Community," in *Arabs in the New World: Studies on Arab American Communities*, ed. S. Abraham and Nabeel

Abraham (Detroit: Center for Urban Studies, Wayne State University, 1983), 164–84.

67. The Office of Refugee Resettlement has a variety of reports on the progress, needs, and numbers of Iraqi refugees (approximately three thousand annually) that have been allowed into the United States since 1991. See their web site at http://www.acf.dhhs.gov/programs/orr/.

68. Barbara Aswad, ed., *Arabic-Speaking Communities in American Cities* (New York: Center for Migration Studies, 1974).

69. Joe Borrajo, "Mine Was a Typically Unusual Family," *Detroit Free Press*, 18 October 1990; Alixia Naff, The Arab Americans (New York: Chelsea House Publications, 1988).

70. Based on recent observations in the Southend community.

71. Participant observation and frequent visits to the community confirm these details.

72. Barbara Aswad, public lecture, July 1994.

73. Hassoun, "Dearborn Arab-American Community Restaurant and Tourist Guide."

74. See the *Detroit News*, 28 August 1994.

75. The *Detroit News* and *Free Press*, 27 August 1994.

76. Sengstock, "Traditional and Nationalist Identity in a Christian Arab Community"; Mary C. Sengstock, *Chaldean Americans: Changing Conceptions of Identity* (Staten Island, N.Y.: Center for Migration Studies, 1982).

77. J. Ghannem, "Arab Americans: All the Problems but None of the Attention," *Quill* 79 (1991): 38.

78. A. H. Salah and A. Jabara, "Blacks and Iraqis Collide in Detroit," *Freedomways* (Nov. 3, 1983): 179–85.

79. Confidant interviews, *Metropolitan Detroit*, R. Hassoun, 1991–93.

80. EPA representative, conversation with author, March 1993.

81. Hassoun, "Bioanthropological Perspective."

82. Ibid.; Hassoun, "Greater Cleveland Arab-American Needs Assessment"; and Rosina Hassoun, "Arab-American Health and the Process of Coming to America: Lessons from the Metropolitan Detroit Area," in *Arabs in America: Building a New Future*, ed. Michael W. Suleiman (Philadelphia: Temple University Press, 1999), 157–76.

83. Hassoun, "Bioanthropological Perspective."

84. Hassoun, "Arab-American Health."

85. Ibid.

86. See Hassoun, "Bioanthropological Perspective," and Hassoun, "Greater Cleveland Arab-American Needs Assessment."

87. For an overview of Arabic language maintenance in America, see Aleya Rouchy, ed., *The Arabic Language in America* (Detroit: Wayne State University, 1992).

88. See note 9.

For Further Reference

Abraham, Nabeel. "The Yemeni Immigrant Community of Detroit: Background, Emigration, and Community." In *Arabs in the New World: Studies on Arab-American Communities*, edited by S. Abraham and Nabeel Abraham, 109–34. Detroit: Center for Urban Studies, Wayne State University, 1983.

Abraham, Sameer. "Community in Metropolitan Detroit." In *The Arab World and Arab Americans: Understanding a Neglected Minority*, edited by Sameer Abraham and Nabeel Abraham, 22–33. Detroit: Wayne State University Center for Urban Studies, 1981.

——. "Detroit's Arab-American Community: A Survey of Diversity and Commonality." In *Arabs in the New World: Studies on Arab-American Communities*, edited by S. Abraham and Nabeel Abraham, 84–86. Detroit: Center for Urban Studies, Wayne State University, 1983.

Abraham, Sameer Y., and Nabeel Abraham. *Arabs in the New World: Studies on Arab-American Communities*. Detroit, Mich.: Wayne State University Center for Urban Studies, 1983.

Abraham, S. Y., Nabeel Abraham, and Barbara Aswad. "The Southend: An Arab Muslim Working-Class Community." In *Arabs in the New World: Studies on Arab-American Communities*, edited by S. Abraham and Nabeel Abraham, 164–84. Detroit: Center for Urban Studies, Wayne State University, 1983.

Abu-Laban, Sharon McIrvin, and Baha Abu-Laban. "Teens Between: The Public and Private Spheres of Arab-Canadian Adolescents." In *Arabs in America: Building a New Future*, edited by Michael W. Suleiman, 113–28. Phialadelphia: Temple University Press, 1999.

Ameri, Anan, and Yvonne Lockwood. *Arab Americans in Metro Detroit: A Pictorial History*. Chicago: Arcadia Publishing, 2001.

Aswad, Barbara, ed. *Arabic-Speaking Communities in American Cities*. New York: Center for Migration Studies, 1974.

Bawardi, Hani. "Arab Immigrants in Flint, Michigan: The Case of Merchants in the Inner City." M.A., University of Michigan, Flint 1997.

Borrajo, Joe. "Mine Was a Typically Unusual Family." *Detroit Free Press*, 18 October 1990.

Christoff, Chris. "Police Report: Apology on the Way for Stirring Fear, Bias." *Detroit Free Press*, 25 October 2001.

Daniels, Roger, and Otis L. Graham. *Debating American Immigration, 1882–Present*. Boulder, Colo.: Rowman and Littlefield, 2001.

Darden, J. T., R. C. Hill, and J. Thomas. *Detroit: Race and Uneven Development*. Philadelphia: Temple University Press, 1987.

David, Gary. *The Mosaic of Middle Eastern Community in Metropolitan Detroit*. Detroit: United Way Community Services, 1998.

El Badry, S. "The Arab American Market." *American Demographics* 16(1): 22-30.

Etten, William J. *A Citizen's History of Grand Rapids*. Grand Rapids, Mich.: A. P. Johnson for the Campau Centennial Committee, 1926. Available on-line at http://www.rootsweb.com/~mikent/etten1926/cosmopolitan.html.

Gaurilovich, Paul. "Detroit's Arab-American Community Is North America's Largest." *Detroit Free Press*, 18 October 1990, 2E.

Ghannem, J. "Arab Americans: All the Problems but None of the Attention." *Quill* 79 (1991): 38.

Hassoun, George, and L. Louise Hassoun. *The ABC's of Middle Eastern Cooking*. Camas, Wash.: Bellgraphics, 1989.

Hassoun, Rosina. "Arab-American Health and the Process of Coming to America: Lessons from the Metropolitan Detroit Area." In *Arabs in America: Building a New Future*, edited by Michael W. Suleiman, 157–76. Philadelphia: Temple University Press, 1999.

———. "Bioanthropological Perspective of Hypertension in Arab Americans in Metropolitan Detroit." Ph.D. diss., University of Florida, 1995.

———. *Dearborn Arab-American Community Restaurant and Tourist Guide.* Dearborn: Ford Motor Company and the Michigan Equity Program and the City of Dearborn with the Arab Community Center for Economic and Social Services, 1994.

———. *The Greater Cleveland Arab-American Needs Assessment Final Report.* Cleveland: Arab-American Community Center For Economic and Social Services in Ohio (AACCESS-Ohio), 2001.

Hiltermann, Joost. "Abu Jamal: A Palestinian Urban Village." In *Labor and the Women's Movement in the Occupied Territories,* edited by E. Burke, 364–67. Princeton, N.J.: Princeton University Press, 1991.

Hitti, Phillip. *The Syrians in America.* New York: George H. Doran, 1924.

Hughes, Paul. "Selling Arab-America to the Tourism Industry: Efforts Underway to Take Advantage of Large Population Concentrations." Arab American Business, August 2001. On-Line version available at: http://www.arabamericanbusiness.com/issue10_august/marketing.htm

Khalidi, Walid, ed. *All That Remains: The Palestinian Villages Occupied and Depopulated by Israel in 1948.* Berkeley: University of California Press, 1992.

McCarus, Ernest, ed. *The Development of Arab-American Identity.* Ann Arbor: University of Michigan Press, 1994.

Michigan Department of Public Health. *Minority Health in Michigan.* Lansing: Michigan Department of Public Health, 1988.

Naff, Alixia. *The Arab Americans.* New York: Chelsea House Publications, 1988.

Orfalea, Gregory. *Before the Flames: Quest for the History of Arab Americans.* Austin: University of Texas Press, 1988.

Peters, Emyrs L. "Aspects of Rank and Status among Muslims in Lebanese Villages." In *Mediterranean Countrymen,* edited by J. Pitt-Rivers. The Hague: Mouton, 1963.

———. "Shifts in Power in a Lebanese Village." In *Rural Politics and Change in the Middle East,* edited by Richard Antoun and E. Harik. Bloomington, Ill.: Indiana University Press, 1972.

Rouchy, Aleya, ed. *The Arabic Language in America.* Detroit: Wayne State University Press, 1992.

Salah, A. H., and A. Jabara. "Blacks and Iraqis Collide in Detroit." *Freedomways* (1983): 179–85.

Samhan, Helen Hatam. "Not Quite White: Race Classification and the Arab-

American Experience." In *Arabs in America: Building a New Future*, edited by Michael W. Suleiman, 209–26. Phialdelphia: Temple University Press, 1999.

Sengstock, Mary C. *Chaldean Americans: Changing Conceptions of Identity.* Staten Island, N.Y.: Center for Migration Studies, 1982.

———. "Traditional and Nationalist Identity in a Christian Arab Community." *Sociologist Analysis* 35 (1974): 201–10.

Suleiman, Michael W. "Introduction: The Arab American Immigrant Experience." In *Arabs in America: Building a New Future*, edited by Michael W. Suleiman, 1–21. Philadelphia: Temple University Press, 1999.

Terry, Janice J. "Community and Political Activism among Arab Americans in Detroit." In *Arabs in America: Building a New Future*, edited by Michael W. Suleiman, 241–54. Philadelphia: Temple University Press, 1999.

Zogby, John. *Arab America Today: A Demographic Profile of Arab Americans.* Washington, D.C.: Arab American Institute, 1990.

Index

A

Abraham, Nabeel, 15, 22

Abraham, Spencer, 5, 35

Abu-Lughud, Abrahim, 37

acculturation, 25, 35, 52, 53, 54, 55–56, 59, 60, 61

activism, scholarly, 37–38

African Americans, 5, 29, 43, 49, 54, 57; Arab-American relations with, 31, 32, 50, 72 (n. 78)

Al Bassa, 20, 35–36, 59

Algeria, 17

American Druze Foundation, 29, 58

American Friends (Quakers), 19

Ann Arbor, Michigan, 12, 37–39, 59

anti-terrorist laws, 3, 24

Arab Community Center for Economic and Social Services (ACCESS), 48, 49, 50, 60, 65, 68 (n. 19); Community Health Center, 3, 4

Arab counties, 6, 17

Arab Americans, 7, 8, 17; affluent, 13, 14, 20, 48, 50, 52, 58, 59, 84; congressmen, 5; demographics, 5, 8–12, 70 (n. 49); and exercise, 54; males, 21, 31, 53; professional, 12, 55; U.S. Census Bureau racial/ethnic classification of, 6; women, 46, 48, 52, 53, 60; working-class, 13, 14, 24, 45, 47

Arab American Institute (AAI) Foundation, 8

Arab American studies, 22

Arab-American National Museum, 66

Arab and Chaldean Council (ACC), 7, 50, 60, 65

Arab Jewish populations, 7

Arab League, 58

Arab settlement patterns, in Michigan, 21–25

Arab World: brain drain from, 38, 58; ethnic and religious diversity in, 7, 52, 60; urbanization in, 19

unions, 2
University of Michigan, 12, 38, 59;
    Center for Near Eastern and
    North African Studies, 12
urban lifestyle, adjustment to, 51

V

veiling, 46
villages, 20, 33, 46, 49, 51, 54, 55;
    intermarriage in, 35, 36, 44;
    Lebanese, 18, 19, 69 (n. 23);
    Palestinian, 69 (n. 25), 71 (n. 51)

W

Warren Ave , 44, 48, 84
Warren, Michigan, 12, 13, 14
Washington, D.C., 10
Wayne County, 8, 11, 57
Wayne State University, 22

West Bank, 12, 13, 19, 20
West Michigan, Arab American com-
    munity, 39
"white flight," 43
Woody's Oasis Restaurant, 35
World War I, 42

Y

Yemen, 1, 2, 7, 12, 14, 17, 43, 46; civil
    war in, 43; Hadramaut, 58; North
    and South, 44; unification of, 44
Yemeni, 1, 2, 12, 14, 17, 42, 43, 44,
    47, 57, 56, 58

Z

Zamel, Wadih (Woody), 35
Zogby, John, 5, 8
Zogby International, 5, 8